Contemporary American Theologies

Contemporary American Theologies

A Critical Survey

Deane William Ferm

The Seabury Press • New York

1981
The Seabury Press
815 Second Avenue
New York, N.Y. 10017

Printed in the United States of America

Library of Congress Cataloging in Publication Data

Ferm, Deane William, 1927–
    Contemporary American theologies.

    Bibliography: p. 168
    Includes index.
    1. Theology, Doctrinal—United States—History—
20th century. I. Title.
BT30.U6F4   230'.0973   81-5678
ISBN 0-8164-2341-5   AACR2

To My Mother
And
In Memory Of My Father

Table Of Contents

Preface

My purpose in writing this book has been threefold First, I have summarized the major trends in contemporary American Christian theology. Second, I have referred to some of the significant literature representative of these new developments. I realize that each chapter could be expanded into a book. For this reason I have included a brief bibliography in the hopes that the reader will want to explore further in these areas. Third, I have suggested ways in which I believe American Christian theology can best meet the challenges of our time. I have sought above all for clarity and simplicity.

The judgments I have made regarding recent theological trends can best be understood with reference to two equally important dimensions of our lives: "inner history" and "outer history." We all have our unique inner history. My mother is not your mother. My background is not your background. Each group of people has its own inner history: blacks, women, Swedes, Catholics, and so on. This inner history is crucial for discovering one's identity as an individual and as a member of a particular group. But we also have an outer history which we all share. We are children of one God. We are inhabitants of the same planet earth. We are human beings. We all have our hopes and frustrations, our dreams and fears. We all want to love and be loved. My chief criticism of many of the theologies of the 1960s and 1970s is that they have rightly been concerned with their inner histories, but in so doing they have often neglected the outer history which we all share. The result has been a fractured faith.

A second criterion concerns the central theological task. I believe that the number one problem for the theologian remains the problem of God. Is God real? What is the character of ultimate reality? Is the universe friendly, antagonistic, or indifferent? Many of the theologies of the 1960s and 1970s have correctly been concerned with God's activity but have neglected God's nature. I believe that who God is, is as important as what God does. The one without the other also results in a fractured faith. Both of these criteria I develop in the final chapter where I suggest the direction in which I think theology should move.

In order to understand what has happened in American Christian theology since 1960, one needs to have some knowledge of theological developments prior to this period. Therefore, I have included an introductory chapter which summarizes American Protestant theology from around the beginning of this century to the 1960s. Since the early 1960s, theology has been decidedly ecumenical in character; hence, both Catholic and Protestant theologians are included.

Admittedly, in summarizing these theological movements I write as an outsider attempting both to understand and to interpret. I do not deny my own bias. I write as one who is deeply concerned about the critical problems plaguing the human race. I strongly believe that a major task for theologians is to enter into dialogue with one another to help heal the fractures of faith and society, break down human-made divisions between oppressor and oppressed, and further the search for that larger dimension of religious and human experience that unites us as sisters and brothers and as children of the living God.

I wish to thank the editors of the following journals for permission to use copyright material already published: *Religion in Life* (Autumn 1975; Winter 1980); *Choice* (February 1980); *Scottish Journal of Theology* (Vol. 34, No. 2 April 1981). Readers of my articles which appeared in *The Christian Century* (March 1972; May 1978) will recognize here some ideas previously expressed in this journal.

I am indebted to many people too numerous to mention for helping to shape the views I express in this book. There are two people without whose help this project would never have been completed. My loyal secretary, Mary Miller, has patiently typed several drafts and has been a great help in eliminating many grammatical errors. My wife, Debra, is in a real sense the coauthor. Not only have her superior literary skills improved the quality of my writing, but even more important, her constant love and encouragement have been, and continue to be, my greatest inspiration. But I absolve her from all responsibility for my ideas!

Deane William Ferm
South Hadley, Massachusetts
January, 1981

1

Protestant Theology: 1900–1960

Protestantism in the twentieth century has faced upheavals in the intellectual, economic, and social spheres as momentous as those of the early sixteenth century. In both periods Christianity could not afford to remain indifferent to these dramatic changes if it were to continue to be a vital force in human history. In order to understand why recent American Protestant theology is in some respects so unlike its earlier forms, we must be cognizant of the shape of modern thought.

The principal cause of the new approach to theological thinking in modern times has been the scientific revolution. This movement challenged the basic affirmations of the Christian faith: the existence of a personal God, the deity of Jesus Christ, the assurance of a life to come. The world of the twentieth century has been one in which nothing could be taken for granted, a world in which the only certainty has been that there is no certainty. The bond between the old religious beliefs and the new intellectual ideas was ruptured and perhaps irreparably broken.

The traditional western Christian world view presupposed a universe both paternalistic and dualistic in character. God stood over against humanity and Christ was the reconciler of the two. Christ was able, in a unique and final way, to bridge the gap between the divine and the human, the supernatural and the natural. The term *supernatural* points to an order of reality (God) beyond humanity which cannot be known through human initiative. The supernatural order can become known only if that reality, that is, God, is revealed through divine intervention. It is precisely this kind of dualism based on knowledge via revelation which seems alien to the world view bequeathed by the scientific revolution.

It is impossible to date precisely when people began to think differently about themselves and their world. Some historians suggest that the change started as early as 1451 with the invention of printing, others, in 1543 with the publication of the *Revolution of The Heavenly Bodies* by Copernicus. Some cite twelfth-century roots while others think that the change began as late as the seventeenth century. At any rate, an intellectual movement began several centuries ago which slowly and painfully swept across the western world and drastically reshaped human life in its philosophical, social, political, and economic aspects. However, not until the twentieth century did this movement seriously affect humanity's religious convictions.

The principal feature of the scientific revolution is the inductive method of inquiry. This method makes two major assumptions in the search for authentic knowledge. First, direct observation and experimentation is the most reliable way of learning about any subject matter. This does not mean that one must be able to experience everything personally before one will believe it; this would obviously be impossible. Rather, the assumption is that one will not accept any truth as valid unless either one has experienced it or one can trust the observations of someone else. In those areas such as history and anthropology where direct knowledge cannot be attained, one will put confidence in those scholars who have made a thorough study in that particular sphere of inquiry and who have constructed their theories in an orderly manner. Obviously this first principle is not perfect; no assumption is.

The second assumption is that rational analysis is the best judge of the reliability of knowledge. Not only must something be directly experienced by the observer or by someone considered trustworthy, but also it must make sense in terms of the observer's previous information. There must be a coherent pattern between what is already known and what is as yet unknown. No belief can be accepted which is inherently inconsistent with other beliefs or which eludes rational inquiry. Clear thinking is dependent on a harmonious combination of the present with the past. Naturally, with our limited knowledge, one belief does not always harmonize with another. For example, the two theories of light (wave length and corpuscular) seem irreconcilable. The underlying assumption, however, is that the conflict is on the surface. Eventually an underlying principle will be discovered to reconcile all apparent discrepancies.

The hard-fought victory achieved by the scientific method is that truth must be found and tested by human experience and inductive thinking. One's comprehension of truth changes as one's knowledge increases. Religious faith for many modern believers has come to be understood more as a working hypothesis based on reason and experience which gives meaning to life than as a set of revealed truths about the universe which are eternal in character.

In general, Protestant theology has been characterized by three different responses to the scientific revolution: liberalism, conservatism, and neo-orthodoxy. Although advocates of these three positions may still be found today, their influence as major schools of thought was dominant earlier in this century and certainly prior to the 1960s. It is important that we give some attention to each of these movements.

LIBERALISM

The term Protestant liberalism is generally used to refer to that Protestant school of thought which believed that a reinterpretation of the Christian message in accordance with the modern scientific world view was necessary. Liberals claimed that Christianity must harmonize with the contemporary ways of thinking if it were to be relevant to the modern believer.

Perhaps the most important theological forerunner of religious liberalism was the German theologian Friedrich Schleiermacher (1768-1834). Schleiermacher reacted strongly against the intellectualism of his day which tended to view Christianity as a series of propositions rather than as a living relationship with God. He attacked the "cultured despisers" of religion who identified the Christian faith with dogmas and beliefs. He claimed that religion is the feeling of absolute dependence on God and that the goal of Christianity is to experience fully this God-consciousness as Christ himself had done. The extent of his God-consciousness distinguishes Christ from other humans who sin when they choose not to be aware of God. Redemption represents the healing of the divine-human relationship. According to Schleiermacher there is no sharp division among God, Christ, humanity, and the world; they are all dimensions of a continuous spectrum. The encounter with God is the beginning and the end of the Christian life and faith. Doctrines, he once said, must be extracted from the inward experience of Christian people. By the early part of the twentieth century the teachings of Schleiermacher and his followers had coalesced into a definite theological current within Protestantism. Underlying Protestant liberalism are four basic affirmations.

First, liberals stressed the importance of the inductive method of inquiry which was proving to be so successful for progress in other areas of human endeavor. Religious faith must make sense to one's best experience and reason. Faith in God and Christ could not be separated into a special category of revelation that avoided the usual tests of inductive inquiry and personal verification. Liberalism affirmed that questions which affect human destiny need to have modern answers and that the method that had succeeded in the sciences could work as well in the area of religion.

This meant, for example, that the scientific approach to biblical study entailed using the same tests of truth and verification necessary for any other book. Biblical criticism was not new to the twentieth century, especially "Lower Criticism," that is, textual study aimed at reconstructing as accurately as possible the form and content of the original autographs. Efforts in this area predated even the Reformation of the sixteenth century. The twentieth century witnessed the culmination of a later development, that is, "Higher Criticism," which asked the deeper questions about the character and purpose of these writings. Queries were raised about the authorship of the books of the Bible, the authenticity of these documents, the theological bias of the writers, and the meaning of the various passages. This kind of inquiry raised doubts about a whole host of assumptions concerning the Bible that had heretofore been for the most part accepted uncritically, including the authenticity of biblical writings and even the role of biblical authority.

A second feature of Protestant liberalism was its reliance upon experience, not the Bible, as the primary authority. Here experience should be understood to encompass the total spectrum of human life including, of course, the Bible as one aspect of this continuum. It encompasses both the personal and social dimensions. Liberals considered reason to be the tool for organizing and articulating experience and knowledge in a coherent and comprehensive way. The Bible attains its authority, not because of special divine sanction, but because it is a record of human witness to the living God. The Bible is a human document which contains many different ideas, practices, and customs of people who claimed to know God. This knowledge is potentially available to all people. Liberals insisted that such a view of the Bible makes it more real and vital than ever. Morton Enslin writes of the liberal's belief in the Bible:

> It is the record of centuries of achievement and pilgrimage of men and women like himself confronted with the tasks and problems of life. In the course of the years they made many discoveries, gained many insights. It is to him a priceless heritage of the past, and in it he finds much that aids him in his constant search for the gold of life. He is not in the slightest surprised to find it not infrequently self-contradictory were it to be regarded as one book. He knows that it is nothing of the sort but rather a library written by many men over the period of a thousand years. He is not surprised at differences and contradictory points of view . . . When he is challenged by the brash, "So you don't believe the Bible," he is inclined, after perhaps a moment of annoyance at what appears to him bad manners and poor taste, to answer: "I love it, and that seems to me vastly more important."[1]

The liberals judged Christ to be God's supreme revelation. This affirmation was rooted in their experience of God, which may or may not come through reading the Bible. When they declared that religious experience is basic and universal, they were not suggesting that all religions were equal, but insisting that ultimately everyone must develop one's own faith from personal experience rather than the arbitrary testimony of others or the dogmatic acceptance of divine revelation.

A third feature of liberal thought was the stress placed on continuity between God and humanity, reason and revelation. Liberals rejected dualistic thinking which usually disqualified religious beliefs *a priori* from the usual tests of rational inquiry and personal confirmation. Liberalism insisted that truth is one. The problem of divine nature is also by analogy the problem of human nature. Truth cannot be compartmentalized. The ways human beings learn about themselves are the ways they learn about God.

Religious liberalism's advocacy of continuity can be noted in its attitude toward the doctrine of evolution. When Charles Darwin published his *Origin of Species* in 1859 and the *Descent of Man* in 1871, the response from orthodox Christians was quick and denunciatory. What Darwin had suggested, among other things, was that human life had evolved from the lower animals through a process of natural selection and the survival of the fittest. Although this teaching was not new, Darwin was able to amass a great amount of evidence in its favor.

His claim was a threat to orthodox Christianity because evolution seemed to deny the unique status of the human being as a special creature of God. For liberals, however, Darwin's teaching served to underscore the continuity of humanity with other aspects of God's creation and in no way detracted from God's role as creator. *That* God created the world and everything therein is more important than *how* God created it.

Finally, liberals stressed human potential to overcome personal inadequacies and the shortcomings of the social order. They believed that to some extent one can learn about God as one can learn about oneself. One can know the truth to a degree. One can change the world for the better. To be sure, human beings are not infallible nor without sin; they will always be limited in their knowledge and will often use information for selfish purposes. But people do not solve their problems by simply confessing their ignorance nor by making a fetish out of their selfishness. Rather, they should acknowledge their finitude honestly and humbly and then proceed with the task of inquiry and social reform. Liberalism stressed human potential for good rather than an innate tendency toward evil. It understood the essence of Christianity to be the love of God and humanity. Liberals believed that God and humanity are partners and emphasized the joyous and healthy-minded dimensions of human life. To quote Floyd Ross:

> It is one of the tragedies of Christian history that the men who determined the theological pattern or mood for the majority of Christians were men who through a certain combination of endowment and environment lived in the sense that they had quarreled with God. A Socrates or an Eckhart would have appreciated the comment of Thoreau who, when asked on his deathbed whether he had made peace with God, replied: "I was not aware that we had quarreled." Neither Paul, Augustine, nor Luther would have comprehended.[2]

The confidence liberals placed in human potential became evident when they espoused the social gospel. Environment came to be seen as the source of much of humanity's difficulties and imperfections. If the social and physical environment were to be improved, liberals argued, the human situation would likewise improve and the social order would then move closer to reflecting God's will. Human beings as God's children should be able to eliminate many of the injustices and inequalities which exist in society. The strength of the social gospel movement in the early part of the century is a tribute to the confidence liberalism placed in the individual.

The father of the social gospel was Walter Rauschenbusch (1861–1918), for many years professor of church history at Rochester Theological Seminary. Rauschenbusch combined all the major features of the liberal tradition. He stressed the continuity between God and humanity and thereby saw the working of God in and through the labors of humanity. He believed human imperfections to be essentially environmental; one generation corrupted the next. His major writing, *A Theology for the Social Gospel*, provided a rationale for social action which found the purpose of Christianity to be the remaking of society in the image of God:

> We love and serve God when we love and serve our fellows, whom he loves and in whom he lives . . . The new social purpose, which has laid its masterful grip on modern life and thought, is enlarging and transforming our whole conception of the meaning of Christianity.[3]

These features of Protestant liberalism—the scientific spirit, the authority and universality of religious experience, the importance of continuity, and confidence in human nature—represent ways in which liberals attempted to come to terms with the modern world. Although Protestant liberalism as a major theological force began to wane in the 1930s, it retains a following in all the major Protestant denominations.

One of the most significant advocates for Protestant liberalism was Harry Emerson Fosdick (1878–1969). For more than forty years Fosdick was at the forefront of theological and social thinking in America as he brought to this country a prophetic voice of reasoned faith and enlightened hope. Fosdick epitomized Protestant liberalism in three ways. First, he consistently attempted to express the abiding truths of the Christian faith in the changing categories appropriate to the modern world. He knew that no theology could be expressed in final form. As he put it:

> If the day ever comes when men care so little for the basic Christian experiences and revelations of truth that they cease trying to rethink them in more adequate terms, see them in the light of freshly acquired knowledge, and interpret them anew for new days, then Christianity will be finished.[4]

For this reason Fosdick waged a lifelong battle against the fundamentalists and proponents of a static orthodoxy. On the other hand, he also opposed the radicals who threw out the abiding truths of the Christian faith. Without faith in God, his sermons testify, the whole climate of human life would be pointless and the best in one's ethical life would not be possible. Fosdick declared that if God were not personal, then God would have no concern for human life, and "a God of no concern is a God of no consequence." In one of his most moving sermons he declared:

> If we are to have a profound religion we may indeed throw away our old, childish, anthropomorphic ideas of God, but we may not throw away God and leave ourselves caught like rats in the trap of an aimless, meaningless, purposeless universe.[5]

Second, Fosdick stressed the importance of reason in faith. He lived through a period of violent theological upheaval when the winds of doctrine shifted unpredictably, often leaving the individual believer in confusion and turmoil. Fosdick valued reason not because of a naive optimism, but because he himself had struggled with fundamentalism and obscurantism. As he once put it:

> What present-day critics of liberalism often fail to see is its absolute necessity to multitudes of us who would not have been Christians at all unless we could thus have escaped the bondage of the then reigning orthodoxy.[6]

The Christian faith must speak to our deepest insights into our own humanity; otherwise, faith becomes an arbitrary exercise. "Faith and reason," Fosdick insisted, "are not antithetical opposites. They need each other. All the tragic superstitions which have cursed religion throughout its history have been due to faith divorced from reason." [7]

Finally, Fosdick grounded his faith in personal and social experience, in the tragedies and failures, the hopes and dreams of individuals. The most vital thing in religion, he said again and again, is firsthand personal experience. Fosdick was greatly influenced by Walter Rauschenbusch and the social gospel movement, and his intense social concerns are reflected in his writing and preaching. One of humankind's most insistent needs, he wrote in *The Meaning of Service*, is the interpretation of religion in terms of service and the attachment of religion's enormous driving power to the tasks of service. Fosdick believed that both the social and personal dimensions of the Christian faith were essential. But how do we decide which faith? Fosdick answered:

> To take the best insights of them all, to see the incompleteness and falsity in them all, to trust none of them as a whole, to see always that the Reality to be explained is infinitely greater than our tentative, conditioned explanations—that seems to me wisdom.[8]

Harry Emerson Fosdick represented the best in Protestant liberalism.

CONSERVATISM

Liberalism was not the only reaction of Protestant theology to the scientific revolution. The so-called conservatives responded in a totally different way. They proclaimed a set of propositions about the gospel of Jesus Christ which in both form and content remained unchanged despite the shifting human attitudes and world views. This response to the modern world contains much diversity, but for the sake of contrast we shall call it conservatism. Many interpreters have labeled this point of view fundamentalism, but this latter term has been caricatured so badly by liberals as to make it virtually worthless. The term fundamentalism should be reserved for those believers who insisted on a literal interpretation of the words of the Bible. The beginnings of fundamentalism as a self-conscious movement can be dated at 1910 with the publication of a series of pamphlets entitled *The Fundamentals: A Testimony to the Truth*. Fundamentalism later came to be identified with five basic affirmations of the Christian faith:

1. The verbal inspiration of the Bible;
2. The virgin birth of Christ;
3. The substitutionary atonement of Christ for the sins of the world;
4. Christ's bodily resurrection;
5. Christ's second coming.

Although fundamentalism has been and still is a major factor in American religion, its chief advocates have never been leading, well-known theologians. To be sure, fundamentalists and conservatives share many convictions including most of the ones just stated; nevertheless, the leading conservative theologians were not biblical literalists.

Conservatism can be identified as that movement in Protestantism which upheld the inspired content of the entire Bible. Although conservatism had always been present in the history of Protestantism, it emerged as a self-conscious movement early in the twentieth century. Reformation Protestantism had insisted that the Bible was the prime authority for Christian belief and practice, but just what this implied had never been precisely defined. For example, Luther had made distinctions among parts of the Bible in terms of their relative value without in any way denying the primary authority of scripture. Conservatives were reluctant to make such distinctions, preferring to state that God is the author of the entire Bible. Whereas Luther stressed the spirit of the words of the Bible—the Bible is the "cradle of Christ"—as his basis for biblical authority, conservatives stressed the doctrinal content of biblical authority. While they admitted the possibility of textual errors inserted during the copying and translation of the Bible, conservatives reaffirmed the divine authorship and the objectivity of revelation. They rejected Higher Criticism which might question some of the basic divinely revealed propositions. For the conservatives, criticism of scripture in such a fashion is to apply human standards to divine authorship. It is significant that the conservatives accused the liberals of anti-intellectualism when the latter minimized the objective nature of the Christian revelation and gave priority to human experience.

What are some of these propositions which conservatives thought essential to the biblical proclamation and which the liberals had relegated to secondary importance? The major doctrines of early Protestantism—the sovereignty of God, the uniqueness of Jesus Christ, the priesthood of all believers—were reaffirmed by the conservatives. Like the fundamentalists, conservatives retained certain propositions about Christ himself, including belief in the deity of Christ and the virgin birth. Liberals, while continuing to focus on Christ, chose to stress his ethical teachings and considered him to be different only in degree from other prophets and human beings. To the conservatives this represented a denial of the uniqueness of the Christian faith. For them, God was revealed in Christ in a way in which God has never been revealed in any other person. Jesus is "very God of very God," the second person of the Trinity. This is the whole point of the incarnation, that is, God in the flesh. For the conservatives the proposition of the deity of Christ was indispensable.

One way of assuring this uniqueness was to assert the virgin birth of Christ as recorded in the gospels of Matthew and Luke. Christ was born of the Virgin Mary with the Holy Spirit as his father, and to deny this historical fact was to deny the authority of the Bible. Liberals tended to minimize the importance of the virgin birth; Schleiermacher said that it was superfluous. But for the conservatives this doctrine was crucial for it preserved the gulf between God and humanity. To deny the virgin birth, that is, to make Christ corrupt, would be as unthinkable as it would be to accept the doctrine of evolution and thereby reject the sharp difference between humanity and the rest of God's creation.

The conservatives also affirmed the bodily resurrection of Jesus Christ while liberals chose to emphasize the teachings of Jesus rather than his resurrection. Liberals maintained that the modern world view cast doubt upon a resurrection from the dead, while conservatives argued from biblical testimony that it is an historical fact that Jesus appeared to his disciples and to others after his death and was recognized by them.

Also central to the conservative position was the belief in the substitutionary atonement of Jesus for the sins of the world, that is, that Christ died for the sins of humanity. He substituted his life for the human race, thus was sin forgiven and the reconciliation of creator and creature, lost with original sin, reestablished. Christ is not only a moral example for believers to imitate, He is God making the supreme sacrifice in order that humanity might be redeemed. Most conservatives also believe in a second coming of Jesus Christ in bodily form to judge the human race. Christ who had died and was raised from the dead shall reappear, as the Bible prophesied. Conservatives believed that the return of Christ would right the wrongs of an evil world and reward the faithful.

One of the leading conservative theologians was J. Gresham Machen (1881−1937), for many years a professor of Greek New Testament at Princeton Theological Seminary. He was often accused by the liberals of being a fundamentalist, but he rejected this designation, and in fairness to him, it must be said that he was not a biblical literalist. He subsequently withdrew from Princeton Seminary to establish Westminster Seminary in Philadelphia. In his most notable book, *The Virgin Birth of Christ*, he defended the major doctrines of conservatism and concluded:

The New Testament presentation of Jesus is not an agglomeration, but an organism; and of that organism the virgin birth is an integral part. Remove the part, and the whole becomes harder and not easier to accept; the New Testament account of Jesus is not convincing when it is not taken as a whole. Only one Jesus is presented in the Word of God; and that Jesus did not come into the world by ordinary generation, but was conceived in the womb of the virgin by the Holy Ghost.[9]

Although conservatism continued to be a vigorous intellectual force in the life of Protestantism, it mellowed over the years as it confronted continuously the demands of an alien secular world. It grudgingly accepted some of the basic conclusions of Higher Criticism. While there were conservatives who refused to compromise the major tenets, most of their leading theologians modified their views without departing from the fundamental insistence on the authority of the Bible. This conviction has remained the core affirmation of conservative Protestantism.

Liberalism also changed its original emphasis, especially its rather optimistic view of human nature. World War I and the chaos that it caused in the social order had a devastating effect on the liberalism of the earlier period. Although this movement never believed in inevitable human progress onward and upward, it did place confidence in human nature's ability to tame the natural world and solve the problems of the environment. World War I shattered that hope. It was no longer possible to affirm that human nature was good and rational, without also acknowledging that it was evil and irrational. The social disorder of the 1920s created an atmosphere of pessimism about human possibilities that bordered on helplessness and despair—an atmosphere which was ideally suited to existentialism and especially the views of the Danish philosopher Sören Kierkegaard (1813–1853). From the human point of view, history no longer seemed to have meaning or purpose. World War I did not make the world safe for democracy, but rather made it receptive to totalitarian regimes.

The chief fault of liberalism had been its desire to harmonize the Christian faith with the scientific world view and all its prejudices without questioning whether that world view was defective. Fosdick sensed this weakness in the 1930s when he declared that what Christ does to modern culture is to challenge it. However, his protest was too mild and too late in the rising chorus of voices in Protestant theological circles then beginning to assert that the claims of Christ were radically different than the assumptions of the modern era, that the task of the Christian faith is to judge this world and not to join it, and that either this world is meaningless or else it must find its meaning in a transcendent source, namely, God.

NEO-ORTHODOXY

The major Protestant theology from the late 1930s to the late 1950s has been labeled in various ways: Neo-Protestantism, the New Reformation, Dialectical Theology. The most common designation has been neo-orthodoxy. Its chief concern was the deliberate attempt to return to the teachings of the early Reformers, particularly Luther and Calvin. The theologians representing this position were convinced that liberal Protestantism had perverted its heritage and changed the Christian faith into a religion different from that which was intended by the early Reformers. Theirs was a protest against liberalism, but not an affirmation of conservatism, although they held to some beliefs to which conservatives also subscribed. Further, this new movement was essentially a European phenomenon—virtually all of its original leaders were German, Swiss, or English. Its influence on American theology was felt mainly in the theological seminaries and among the intelligentsia and less in the local congregations. It did not begin to dominate in the United States until the effects of the depression of the early 1930s began to take their toll on the human spirit.

Neo-orthodoxy traces its beginnings as a self-conscious movement to Karl Barth (1886–1968), the Swiss theologian who published an interpretation of the Book of Romans in 1918. In this commentary he urged a return to the original Lutheran doctrine of salvation not by works but by faith. This plea won a warm response among European theologians who had lost confidence in human righteousness and self-sufficiency.

There is one major theme which indicates the significant contrast between Protestant liberalism and neo-orthodoxy and explains in large part why the two came to contrary understandings of the Christian faith. Are God and the human being dissimilar with one another or are they alike? Is there a qualitative difference or is the separation one of degree? The answer to these questions has led to a continuing dialogue in the life of the church. In the early church Tertullian upheld the division between God and humanity and insisted that Athens (human speculation) had nothing to do with Jerusalem (divine revelation): one must believe even though it may seem absurd! On the other hand, Clement of Alexandria did not separate faith and knowledge but insisted that "the river of truth is one and streams flow into it on this side and that."

One can with a fair degree of accuracy predict a theologian's views on a great many related issues if one knows that person's stand on this issue of discontinuity versus continuity. The former proclaims the transcendence or "otherness" of God; the latter emphasizes God's immanence, or "nearness." The first believes in a special revelation which God has vouchsafed to the human race in a unique way; the second defends a general revelation which is available to all people. The former separates faith and reason as unrelated and agrees with Barth that "there can be no Christian philosophy, for if it is Christian it is not philosophy, and if it is philosophy, it is not Christian."[10] The latter looks upon faith and reason as partners in building upon one another. The one stresses divine initiative, the other human initiative. The first sees truth in terms of irreconcilable paradoxes; the second seeks for coherence in relating all forms of truth. The former assumes a radical difference between the Christian faith and the other religions of the world and with the secular realm. The latter seeks for a rapprochement with the other religions and with the values of secular society. The one defends a divorce between what is Christian and non-Christian; the other tends to baptize all forms of insights and label them Christian.

Neo-orthodoxy took its stand on the side of discontinuity. What is more, this school of thought derived from this assumption certain theological affirmations which it regarded as imperative for a proper understanding of the Christian faith. Five doctrines summarize the essence of neo-orthodoxy. Although this new movement agreed with conservatism in proclaiming this discontinuity between God and humanity, it disagreed by affirming these five theses as general principles and not as rigid propositions. Conservatism was more susceptible to becoming frozen to specific intellectual formulations of its basic teachings than was neo-orthodoxy which was much more fluid in expressing its convictions.

First, neo-orthodoxy affirmed the unity and authority of the Bible. In the Bible is to be found a Drama of Salvation in which God appears not only as the stage manager of the drama, but also as the chief actor. The Bible is the story of human redemption in which God seeks to bring humanity into a right relationship with God. This bestowal of a supernatural authority on the Bible is the starting point in comprehending the Christian faith. This unique biblical authority is God's own revelation to humankind. The Bible is not the attempt on the part of the individual to know God. Barth insisted:

> It is not the right human thoughts about God which form the content of the Bible, but the right divine thoughts about men. The Bible tells us not how we should talk about God, but what he says to us; not how we find the way to him, but how he has sought and found the way to us; not the right relation in which we must place ourselves to him, but the covenant which he has made with all who are Abraham's spiritual children and which he has sealed once and for all in Jesus Christ.[11]

Barth and his followers were not narrow conservatives in their interpretation of the Bible. They did not consider many parts of the Bible to be scientifically accurate or even historically true and believed that the Bible was written by human beings and not dictated by God. They accepted the results of recent Higher Criticism (for example, Moses was not the author of the first five books of the Bible, there were two stories to Creation, the Gospel of Mark was written before the other three gospels and the Apostle Paul probably wrote only a few of the letters attributed to him in the New Testament). Nevertheless, neo-orthodox theologians declared that there is a supernatural character to the Bible which gives it special status. God "authored" the Bible even though we cannot say precisely how this was done. One must accept the absolute validity of the Bible as the Word of God, as the genuine and supreme criterion of the Christian faith. There was disagreement among neo-orthodox theologians concerning the historicity of such doctrines as the virgin birth and the second coming of Jesus Christ but this did not threaten the unity of their belief in the unique self-disclosure of God in the biblical drama and especially in Jesus Christ.

The Bible, then, is *the authority* for Christians. It is also a *unity*, despite the obvious diversity. Sixty-six (or seventy-two for the Roman Catholics) books written by more than that number of authors are bound to betray a wealth of literary styles, a variety of moral codes, and all types of human characters involved in a multiplicity of situations and circumstances. Nevertheless, all this variety should be seen as beads on the string of a necklace. The thread running throughout the Bible and uniting its diversity is God and God's mighty acts in history.

Second, neo-orthodox thinkers affirmed the uniqueness of the Christian revelation. If the Bible is authoritative and if the climax to the unified biblical drama occurred in the historical event of Jesus the Christ, then the Christian revelation is unique. This is an act of God. There never has been a divine revelation to compare with it and there never will be another like it. The work of salvation has been accomplished. The role of the Christian is to accept gratefully what God has done and to witness to that revelatory event.

One can admit that other religions have deep insights and significant moral truths, but these other religions do not have the divine Christ-event. Therefore, none of them can be considered sufficient in the way that Christianity is true and complete. The Christ-event has to be the starting point and to begin anywhere else is simply false. Barth wrote that "only the man who knows about Jesus Christ knows anything at all about revelation," so that "the confession becomes inevitable that Jesus Christ *alone* is the revelation." Other so-called revelations "we call 'revelations' in a perverted, invalid and loose sense of the concept."[12]

A third feature of neo-orthodox thought is its affirmation of the deity of Christ. The Protestant World Council of Churches originally had as its confession of faith the conviction that "Jesus Christ is God and Savior." This creed was later expanded to state:

> The World Council of Churches is a fellowship of churches which confesses the Lord Jesus Christ as God and Savior according to the Scripture and therefore seeks to fulfill together their common calling to the glory of the one God, Father, Son, and Holy Spirit.

This affirmation neatly ties together the first three doctrines. If the Bible is our special authority and if the biblical drama reaches its climax in God's becoming flesh, that is, the incarnation of Jesus Christ, then Christ is in fact "very God of very God," as the ancient creed proclaimed. He is not just a good man or great prophet or special messenger. He is The Event of history. The Christian faith proclaims that Jesus as God died on the cross for the sins of humanity.

Along with this teaching that Jesus was God went the proclamation of the resurrection. God can never be defeated. The crucifixion of Jesus Christ is not the final chapter, but a necessary sacrificial prelude to the resurrection which climaxed Christ's victory over sin and death. What is important is not so much what Jesus accomplished in his healing and teaching ministry while on earth, but that this individual was raised from the dead through a mighty act of God. Human salvation is achieved through the resurrection and not through Jesus' earthly ministry. One cannot, of course, fully separate Christ's birth, life, death, and resurrection; they are all a part of his total mission. But the focus is on the risen Christ. One begins with the resurrection of the Incarnate Lord. To quote Floyd Filson:

> Biblical theology finds its clearest starting point and interpreting clue in the resurrection of Jesus Christ. . . . The entire New Testament was written in the light of the resurrection fact.[13]

If one does not begin with this proclamation, then one is not a Christian; for to deny the centrality of the resurrection is to negate the deity of Christ and to nullify the supreme authority of the Bible.

Fourth, neo-orthodoxy stressed the sinfulness of humanity. These theologians argued in this fashion: human destiny is to live in a right relationship with God and with one's sisters and brothers. But we fall far short of this goal. We consider ourselves creators rather than accept our place as creatures. Thus, we are sinners when we refuse to recognize our subordinate role. We are no longer the persons that God intended us to be. We have become prisoners unto ourselves and our misuse of reason only serves to sink us deeper into the abyss of self-centeredness. There is nothing that we can do about our sinful condition. Only God can right this terrible wrong, and God has, in fact, done this through Jesus Christ. God offers us a second chance to be what God wants us to be. Our only hope for salvation lies in acknowledging by a sheer act of faith that we are sinful creatures standing in the need of God's mercy. If we do so, we are "justified by faith," and given a new life in and through Jesus Christ.

Neo-orthodoxy found confirmation for its view of human sinfulness in modern existentialism which had its beginnings, in its Christianized form, in the Danish thinker Sören Kierkegaard. He argued that Christianity should begin with the doctrine of sin, for this conviction emphasizes the limitation and corruption of human nature. He taught that "the individual existing" is prior to "the individual thinking." One lives before one thinks; therefore, one's reason is but an artificial and distorted construct of one's authentic self. The trouble with the philosophers, said Kierkegaard, is that they construct a system of beliefs and principles which become more important than the human being.

Does not existence antedate one's ideas about existence? Since reason is secondary and easily corrupted, God can be known only through God's own initiative. One can never reason one's way to faith in God; the chasm between God and the individual is too great. As Kierkegaard declared:

> God and man are two qualities between which there is an infinite qualitative difference. Every doctrine which overlooks this difference is, humanly speaking, crazy; understood in a godly sense, it is blasphemy.[14]

Neo-orthodox theologians followed Kierkegaard at another point as well. Kierkegaard described the human encounter with God as precipitated by a feeling of anguish. Only in a time of deep crisis when we despair of ourselves and any meaning in life can we be confronted with the living God. It is this indispensable sense of "sickness unto death" that is the necessary prelude to the divine self-disclosure. Karl Barth, following Kierkegaard, said that we remain anxious until the "Word of God" takes possession of us. In short, neo-orthodox theologians found confirmation for their general theological position in the revival of Kierkegaard's thought which took place earlier in this century.

The neo-orthodox emphasis on human sinfulness found its most eloquent interpreter in Reinhold Niebuhr (1894–1970). Niebuhr had been the pastor of an Evangelical church in Detroit from 1915 to 1928. There he had first-hand acquaintance with the immense social problems of a great industrial complex. He realized the inability of Protestant liberalism, with its optimistic view of the human capacity, to deal effectively with the social predicament. In the late 1920s he became professor of applied Christian ethics at Union Theological Seminary in New York City where for over thirty years he influenced the social teachings of the Protestant churches. Niebuhr's most astute contributions were directed to "the nature and destiny of man," the title of his most famous book. He continuously attacked the complacent conscience of modern believers for their failure to grasp the demonic tendencies of human nature. The sin of pride has so perverted us that it pervades all our interpersonal relationships. Our ethical choices have an absolute imperative, the love of God, but our decisions themselves are relative to the human situation and are thereby subject to distortion and corruption. As a Christian, one has to act in society even though one knows that every action will be tainted by sin. Niebuhr often used paradox—"sin is inevitable but not necessary"—to clarify humanity's ambiguous role. Many intellectuals with no particular relationship to the Christian church found Niebuhr's analysis of the human condition to be more honest and realistic than other alternatives. His influence on twentieth-century Protestant ethical thinking cannot be overemphasized.

The fifth and final doctrine central to neo-orthodoxy follows from the fourth. Human impotence is to be contrasted with God's power, human creaturely status with God's majesty. Christianity needs to rediscover the Calvinistic and Lutheran stress on the sovereignty and transcendence of God. Kierkegaard's infinite qualitative distinction between God and the individual must be preserved, said these theologians. God is Wholly and Holy Other in the sense that nothing human can compare with God. God in a real sense only becomes immanent in the Incarnation, for this is the only way in which God has made the divine saving grace available to humanity. God is the creator and sustainer of this world as well as its redeemer, but the human being only knows of God's threefold activity in the Incarnation. God's immanence is acknowledged by virtue of transcendence and not the other way around.

Neo-orthodoxy was the major Protestant theology for almost three decades. By the early 1960s, however, it had greatly diminished in importance, and although the causes for this collapse are many, perhaps the major reason was its support of a dualistic supernatural theology—a chasm between God and humanity, revelation and reason. It was this "leap of faith" which many modern believers rejected as inconsistent with the modern world view. Neo-orthodoxy assumed the existence of a supernatural order which forever remained beyond the reach of human initiative. It affirmed that a revelation-claim must be accepted as special and beyond the pale of rational and empirical analysis. Such an assumption no longer made sense to many believers in a post-supernatural age. It served to shield the faith from too many soul-searching questions for which this world needed answers. How can the Bible still be our prime authority when there is such wide disagreement as to what constitutes authority itself? Can we continue to assert dogmatically the uniqueness and superiority of the Christian revelation in this time of increasing religious pluralism? Does not faith divorced from reason lead to superstition? If one stressed too much the transcendence of God, can this not become just a way of justifying a particular revelation-claim? These and similar questions had to be answered fairly and squarely on modern terms and on this point neo-orthodoxy was remiss.

One other factor leading to the demise of neo-orthodoxy that should be mentioned is how one confronts the problem of evil. The suggested answer to this problem, which led in part to the birth of neo-orthodoxy, was precisely the opposite from the solution which provoked its death. The origins of neo-orthodoxy lay in part in liberalism's neglect of the evil dimension of human nature. Human beings had to be saved from their worst selves. Since they appeared unable to save themselves, they turned to a transcendent God for salvation. Now, however, neo-orthodoxy died in part because this same evil dimension made it impossible for human beings to believe in a loving, powerful God who would permit such evil as the Holocaust and Hiroshima to happen. Human beings now sought salvation within themselves. What had happened that had led to this rapid shift in theological thinking? It is to this new climate of the 1960s that we now turn.

2
The Secularism of the Sixties

THE SECULAR SPIRIT

Commentators on the American scene are in general agreement that the decade of the 1960s marked an abrupt transition in American history. Eric Goldman has stated that this period "was a watershed as important as the American Revolution or the Civil War in causing changes in the United States."[1] Sidney Ahlstrom declares that

> The decade of the sixties was a time, in short, when the old foundations of national confidence, patriotic idealism, moral traditionalism, and even of historic Judeo-Christian theism, were awash. Presuppositions that had held firm for centuries—even millennia—were being widely questioned. Some sensational manifestations came and went (as fads and fashions will), but the existence of a basic shift of mood rooted in deep social and institutional dislocations was anything but ephemeral.[2]

And William McLoughlin maintains that the drastic reorientation of our sense of values in the 1960s is tantamount to a Fourth Great Awakening.[3]

The general temper of the 1960s can be characterized by the phrase "the domination of the secular spirit." This new dramatic mood had a profound impact on theological thinking. Secular theology succeeded neo-orthodoxy as the major Protestant theological movement of the 1960s. Secularism is the conviction that the only real world for humankind is that of the temporal and transient, a world knowable essentially through the methods of the natural sciences. Anything beyond this world is either unknowable or illusory. Implicitly such a perspective limits the role of theology to the concerns of the spatial-temporal order.

Several factors converged in the early sixties to make the new secularism attractive to the theologians. First, the secular spirit had come to permeate every dimension of human experience. Technological

21

knowledge had proliferated to the extent that the human being seemed capable of tackling and solving almost every conceivable problem. A spirit of buoyant confidence prevailed. Why turn to an unknown God for help when one is quite capable of taking care of oneself? God had become an hypothesis, needed only by those individuals afraid or unwilling to face the real facts of life: human finitude, the contingency of human existence, the relativity of all human judgments and the tentativeness of belief. Nothing should be considered absolute and final, including God. We humans must create our own destiny. God is no longer a reality.

Then, too, the populist spirit had invaded the churches. The individual lay person insisted on taking part in the decision-making process of the church and demanded the right to formulate individual religious views based on his or her personal experience. An inevitable result of the secular spirit in religion has been that the individual has become the prime arbiter in the evaluation of truth-claims, deciding what is true or false, right or wrong, good or bad. Without claiming to be infallible, the individual must nevertheless take responsibility for what he or she chooses to believe.

There are many historical reasons for the development of what has been called "the Renaissance impulse to individuality." Such an analysis would require a thorough investigation of Western political and egalitarian ideals of freedom and independence in their proper historical context. But a major factor has been the scientific revolution, accompanied as it was by the rise of the inductive method of inquiry. The modern believer will no longer accept as true anything which is handed down without first investigating personally and will not determine beliefs primarily on the basis of external authority. This insistence on independence reached its culmination in religion in the early 1960s.

This approach has had a profound impact on the general attitude toward traditional religious institutions and dogmas. Individuals ask: Why do I need to go to church and why my particular church? Why should I believe that only through Jesus Christ can I be saved? Am I not socially conditioned to believe the way I do? What is so unique about the Bible? Why, if there are certain acknowledged contradictions to be found in scripture, should I not conclude that the entire book is unreliable? How do I really know whether there is a God? Paul Tillich, writing in the 1940s, anticipated this trend.

The Protestant message cannot be a direct proclamation of religious truths as they are given in the Bible and in tradition, for the situation of the modern man of today is precisely one of doubt about all this and about the Protestant church itself. The Christian doctrines, even the most central ones—God and Christ, church and revelation—are radically questioned. . . . They cannot in this form be the message of the church to our time. . . . It cannot be required of the man of today that he first accept theological truths, even though they should be God and Christ. Wherever the church in its message makes this a primary demand, it does not take seriously the situation of the man of today and has no effective defense against the challenge of many thoughtful men of our day who reject the message of the church as of no concern for them.[4]

Traditional religion seems inadequate to cope with modern questions because it tends to give ''revealed'' answers which are beyond the pale of rational analysis and empirical confirmation. Moreover, religion offers so many contradictory answers, most of which are not verifiable. Some faiths assert that there are many gods, others that God is spirit. Some declare that she is of feminine gender, others that he is masculine, still others that God is neuter. Some affirm the reality of material substance, others deny it. Within Christianity there is a dispute over the nature of authority, the number and efficacy of the sacraments and how they should be administered and so on. The modern seeker concludes that individual rational inquiry is needed to evaluate such claims if religion is not to degenerate into divisive conflict or purely subjective emotional expression. Christian theology has not escaped this searching scepticism. To quote psychologist Gordon Allport:

In the American Protestant culture perhaps the most significant influence upon religious development is the fact that youth is normally encouraged to question authority. He is expected, if not by his family, at least by his college and by his contemporaries, to scrutinize all established ways of looking at things. He is not only permitted but actively encouraged to find flaws in the school, in the home, in the social system, in the church. For fully two centuries the church has been the favorite target of criticism. . . . The fashion of the times therefore encourages youth to join the attackers rather than the defenders. . . . To reject the church of the parent is one way of stepping forth as an independent adult in a culture where the child is expected to outstrip his parents in occupational, social, and educational accomplishments.[5]

The encouragement of independent thinking has meant a gradual decline in church authority and attendance. In former times when people accepted without question church and clerical authority, the religious institution could exercise great control over its constituency—its behavior as well as its beliefs. Members were told what was true and right and what should be done about it. They believed and sometimes repented. Today this authority is seldom acknowledged except in the conservative churches. In the major Protestant denominations, and even increasingly in the Catholic church, the minister can no longer demand or even expect a congregation to embrace a certain set of convictions or even a particular code of action. The inevitable result is both "situation ethics" and "situation theology." The individual becomes the arbiter. In short, what Sidney Ahlstrom diagnoses as a credibility gap has separated many educated people and their secular style of thinking from traditional forms of religion.[6]

This recession of authority has become the rule rather than the exception in most Protestant churches, an inevitable result of both the modern period and the decentralized form of government in these organizations. The 1960s has seen a similar loss of control in the Roman Catholic church despite its centralized and authoritarian hierarchy. A large number of Catholic believers flout their church's teachings on such matters as regular attendance at mass or the practice of artificial birth control. The Roman church as an organization has begun to awaken to the fact that it must come to terms with the modern world. The late and dearly beloved Pope John XXIII gave official voice to this movement toward independent thinking when in his final encyclical, *Pacem in Terris,* he upheld the integrity of the individual conscience by declaring that every human being has the right "to honor God according to the sincere dictates of his own conscience." In making such an affirmation he was proclaiming a basic Protestant declaration that Martin Luther made famous in his reply at the Diet of Worms, that to go against one's conscience is neither safe nor right. The loss of church authority, together with the increase of critical independent thinking, has led to the decline of traditional religion and the rise of the secular spirit in theology.

Another feature of the 1960s has been the growth of religious pluralism. Dramatic advances in technology during the past few decades, along with improved methods of communication, have caused our planet to shrink to such an extent that an event that happens in what was once considered a remote section of the earth can now have drastic implications thousands of miles away. The possibility of a nuclear war is forcing us to admit our dependence on every other human being and the natural and human barriers which have long divided humankind are now seen to be fragile and fleeting. This global neighborhood has caused the intermingling of peoples of varied cultural, racial, and religious backgrounds.

In the Western world this new understanding among religions has been confined until quite recently to traditions within Christendom and has been the primary cause of the ecumenical movement. Increasing cooperation over the years has led the participating churches to question the validity and importance of their historical differences, to search for a deeper unity, and to concentrate on secular concerns about which agreement can be more easily attained. The ecumenical movement is a significant feature of Protestantism in our day. Denominationalism based on theological differences is rapidly becoming a relic of the past. Pluralism has led to a blurring of historical differences.

The Roman Catholic church in the 1960s also began to acknowledge officially the growth of a Christian pluralism by recognizing other Christian communions as valid in their own right. This was a radical departure from its historical view of Protestantism as heresy and of salvation outside the Roman church as a highly unlikely possibility. This church, under the authority of the pope, viewed itself as the only one established by Christ. As late as 1928 Pope Pius XI in an encyclical entitled "Mortalium Animos" stated that

> There is but one way in which the unity of Christians may be fostered, and that is by furthering the return to the one true Church of Christ by those who are separated from it; for from that one true Church they have in the past fallen away.

It is not surprising in light of the above that Catholics were forbidden to attend early meetings of the World Council of Churches.

This intransigent attitude changed in the 1960s, due primarily to the efforts of Pope John XXIII. In 1959 the pontiff, elected as a transitional leader, decided to convene Vatican II to finish the work of Vatican I which had ended abruptly in 1870 with the beginning of the Franco-Prussian War. The Vatican Council of the early 1960s was in large measure a dramatic acknowledgement of the challenges of the twentieth century. Vatican II met first in 1962 and continued, with two-month working sessions, through 1965. Pope John invited Protestant observers to attend these sessions and he further encouraged Catholic representatives to be present at meetings of the World Council of Churches. Of the statements emanating from Vatican II, none is more encouraging for Catholic-Protestant relations than the decree entitled "On Ecumenism." This document refers to Protestants not as heretics but as "separated brethren whose Churches are used by the Spirit as a means of salvation." It encourages Catholic priests and laymen to meet with their Protestant friends to discuss freely their common Christian faith as well as to work together on community endeavors. Special worship services were sponsored and planned by Catholics and Protestants acting in concert.

Pope John died in 1963 and his successor Paul VI continued the sessions of the Council with the move toward greater intra-church cooperation. When the deliberations of the Council were completed in 1965, a joint working group of Catholics and Protestants established officially by the Catholic Church and the World Council of Churches continued to wrestle with issues of doctrine and worship. At the Fourth Assembly of the World Council in Uppsala in 1968, Roman Catholic theologians were much in evidence, and several of them were made full members of the Faith and Order Commission.

Serious obstacles remain before Catholic and Protestant cooperation can be complete. The most critical difference centers on the locus of authority. The Catholic Church insists that it is God's will that the pope must be the prime authority. Protestants are unanimous in rejecting this claim. Some movement away from the traditional Catholic affirmation appeared to take place at Vatican II in the emphasis on *collegiality,* the sharing of authority between pope and bishops. Other thorny issues of conflict include the Catholic position on the role of the Virgin Mary as comediator with Christ and on the number and significance of the sacraments. Despite these formidable obstacles, however, Catholics and Protestants are on the road toward one ecumenical venture. Indeed, leading Roman Catholic theologian Hans Küng could assert a few years ago that there is no longer a Protestant theology in opposition to a Catholic theology, but rather an emerging ecumenical theology, and that differences between Catholics and Protestants today "are not the traditional doctrinal differences"; rather, they are "traditional basic attitudes which have developed since the Reformation,'' [7] attitudes that should now be overcome.

The significant fact for our purposes is the recognition of a genuine pluralism among Christian groups. However, as yet there has been little indication that rapidly improving transportation and communication will mean a rapprochement with non-Christian religions. There are four major living religions today competing for the allegiance of humanity: Hinduism, Buddhism, Christianity, and Islam. In the 1960s each experienced a revival of interest, projecting continued expansion and development. The Eastern religions in particular have been of great curiosity and fascination to the Western mind. At the same time that these religions are expanding their educational and missionary programs, an American religious amalgamation has occurred at the grass roots. Reflecting on the presidency of John F. Kennedy, William McLoughlin observes that "the election of a Roman Catholic to the presidency in 1960 was a symbol of the end of Protestant hegemony and the beginning of what some historians have called "the post-Protestant era" or "the second disestablishment."[8] Hindus and Moslems have held seats in the Congress, Mormons have been governors of states and members of the President's cabinet, developments that could not have occurred a generation ago. Members of diverse religious groups in increasing numbers are living in the same neighborhoods and sharing their beliefs with one another. This is an inevitable result of technology and a shrinking planet. Today's religious diversity forces humankind to recognize good qualities in other religions as well as their own. It is compelling the believer to realize that the Divine Light, if it shines at all, shines in other faiths and not only in one's own. The claims of individual religions to uniqueness and superiority have begun to melt before the facts of everyday experience. Church members are being forced to restructure their beliefs in a way that cuts across religious traditions and brings to the fore the universal elements which bind people to one another.

Finally, the growth of the civil rights movement in the 1960s and the Vietnam war had a profound impact on theology. Religious and humanitarian concerns merged in an unprecedented way as clergy and lay people of the different churches flocked to the picket lines to dramatize the relevance of their faith to the issues of war and equal rights. Theology became primarily an ecumenical matter of social activism and involvement and theological thinking became largely a reflection on social change. Speculation about ultimate reality in the 1960s came to be considered artificial and unreal. God became the instrument for social change, a further symptom of an emerging secularism in religion.

The "New Secularism" had a profound impact on theological trends in the 1960s. This pervasive secular spirit, with its unbounded confidence in one's ability to solve one's own problems, along with an emerging religious pluralism which tended to blunt traditional sectarian differences, and an emphasis on social action as a religious activity, all converged to influence new theological concerns and directions.

Two theologians are particularly prominent during the period of transition to the secular sixties. Although they are not to be considered "secular theologians," their ideas contributed significantly to the changing theological scene. One of them is Paul Tillich (1886–1965), who emigrated to America in 1933 after being forced by the Nazis to leave his German homeland. Tillich entitled his autobiography *On The Boundary,* and indeed this is the stance from which he spoke and wrote as a Christian. For Tillich, the modern believer has to live in creative tension between faith and doubt, theology and philosophy, revelation and reason, the sacred and the secular, the church and the world. Tillich wants to make contact with the unbeliever to show how the Christian gospel speaks to the human condition. He conceives of God as the "being beyond being" who cannot be defined or categorized, and the Christian proclamation, as the manifestation of the New Being to which Jesus as the Christ bears witness. Faith is one's "courage to be"—the courage to affirm being and meaning despite the threat of non-being and insignificance.

Tillich insists on judging all human assumptions as limited and subject to sin, for only God is beyond corruption. He calls this judgment the "Protestant principle." In essence this principle is another way of expressing the conviction of the early reformers of the sovereignty of God. Only God is supreme; all other institutions, dogmas, and individuals are subject to God alone. Tillich uses the language of both the theologian and philosopher to develop his ideas about the nature of God, the individual, and the world. His unusual breadth of knowledge and his willingness to be receptive to insights from the social and natural sciences made him a respected figure in all segments of the intellectual community. Only the dogmatists of whatever stripe—including some of his own interpreters who distorted certain aspects of his teaching—have failed to appreciate his contributions.

Another theologian whose writings influenced the Protestant theological development of the 1960s is Dietrich Bonhoeffer (1906–1945), a brilliant German theologian who was executed by the Nazis shortly before he would have been freed from prison by the American army. He never wrote a systematic theology, yet his writings became the starting point for a whole new breed of religious thinkers. His ideas are often cryptically presented, such as in the following sentences from his *Letters and Papers from Prison:*

> We are proceeding towards a time of no religion at all; men as they are now simply cannot be religious any more.

> If religion is no more than the garment of Christianity . . . then what is religionless Christianity?

> God is the "beyond" in the midst of our life.

> To be a Christian does not mean to be religious in a particular way . . . but to be a man.

> God is teaching us that we must live as men who can get along very well without him.[9]

Bonhoeffer's writings have been widely quoted in recent years to support almost every conceivable theological position. Briefly, he teaches that God is calling the Christian to a way of living which will not be dependent on the religious and theological trappings of the past. He reaffirms Luther's assertion that the individual is justified not through "religious good works or theology," but through complete trust in God and faithful involvement in the life of the world. Many theologians are more impressed with Bonhoeffer's phrases "man cannot be religious anymore" and "we must learn to live without God" than with his underlying and unyielding commitment to the God who transcends all human forms and institutions.

THEOLOGICAL RESPONSES

The most widely read theological book of the early 1960s was *Honest to God* (1963) by the English theologian John Robinson. This little book, which in substance amounts to a popularization of some of the key ideas of Tillich and Bonhoeffer, is significant not only as a repudiation of neo-orthodoxy, the dominant Protestant theological trend of the 1940s and 1950s, but also as a presentation of theological views more in keeping with the developing secular spirit. Robinson affirms that God can no longer be considered as physically or metaphysically "out there" or "up there" in another supernatural realm. Rather, God is "within," as the ground of our being (Tillich). Theology is

> an analysis of the depth of *all* experience "interpreted by love." . . . A statement is "theological" not because it relates to a particular Being called "God," but because it asks *ultimate* questions about the meaning of existence: it asks what, at the level of *theos*, at the level of its deepest mystery, is the reality and significance of our life.[10]

For Robinson, to speak of God is to speak of the transcendent qualities of human existence, those qualities that touch the most profound depths of reality. To believe in Jesus is not to believe in a person of two distinct natures, divine and human, but to believe in a "man for others" (Bonhoeffer) in whom love has taken over, one who is united with the ground of his existence.

Robinson thus rejects the dualism inherent in neo-orthodoxy which makes God and humanity totally distinct. He affirms the oneness of life, both divine and human, and articulates a view of transcendence, God, and Jesus that is more in harmony with the secular spirit. *Honest To God* received wide acclaim; Robinson had probed a sensitive area. He sought to deal with religious faith in a way compatible with the modern spirit.

Another attempt to come to terms with the secular spirit that gained strength in the 1960s is process theology. This school of thought traces its roots to the philosopher Alfred North Whitehead and theologians Henry Nelson Wieman and Charles Hartshorne. These thinkers contend that all reality must be understood first and foremost as dynamic and constantly in process of change, a view consistent with the modern cosmology and its stress on uncertainty, change, relativity, and growth. God is not a static and unchangeable substance but a creative force which continues to move toward greater fulfillment. Process theologians stress the organic unity of all of life that permeates and integrates God, nature, and humanity, a unity constantly evolving toward greater enrichment and fulfillment. Although in Whitehead's terms God's *primordial* nature is always one and the same, God's *consequent* nature is always in process of development, a view of God aptly described in Hartshorne's phrase "divine relativity." God is dipolar, being both relative and absolute at the same time. God is "that factor in the universe which establishes what-is-not as relevant to what-is, and lures the world toward new forms of realization."[11] Such a view allows for the presence of evil: "Since God is not in complete control of the events of the world, the occurrence of genuine evil is not incompatible with God's benificence toward all his creatures."[12] Process theology, in taking the secular spirit seriously, seeks to make God real for today's believers who live in a world marked by change and uncertainty and who seek a vision of God in harmony with these present day realities. John Cobb and Schubert Ogden are two contemporary theologians who find these insights particularly fruitful. Process theology, in its concern to keep the reality of God both central and palatable to the modern believer, will have a growing influence in the development of an indigenous American theology even though it will probably never receive popular acclaim. It deserves more attention than can be given in this brief summary.

Another important figure, although not strictly a process theologian, is the Roman Catholic thinker Teilhard de Chardin (1881–1955). A philosopher and paleontologist by profession, Teilhard sought to harmonize his Catholic faith with a vision of life as an ever-flowing process toward greater fulfillment culminating in the ultimate Omega of Ecstasy. His masterpiece, *The Phenomenon of Man* (1959), published posthumously since it did not receive official church approval, was an instant success in its optimistic view of a Christian humanism evolving toward an irreversible perfection. Teilhard's influence on Catholic and Protestant theology in the 1960s was profound. He was clearly a theologian ahead of his times.

The theological trend of the early and middle sixties that captured the attention of the widest segment of the American public was the "death-of-God" theology. Its startling affirmations received widespread coverage in the national news media. Even many Americans thoroughly removed from theological interests could not escape the proclamation of the death of God on the cover of *Time* magazine. Although this theology exhibits the usual variety apparent in all ideologies, two convictions stand out. First, these theologians attack the belief in God and anything which smacks of the supernatural. They are convinced that the assumptions of the secular spirit mean that God is dead. Their claim is not that God can no longer be experienced, but that God is not around to be experienced. Moreover, a curious and uncritical affirmation of the centrality of the man Jesus accompanies the proclamation of the death of God. Jesus as "the man for others" is held up as the best model for humanity. He is the one to whom the Christian turns as the ideal of the good life. Jesus serves his neighbor and loves the world and so should we. In this way the death-of-God theologians dubbed themselves "Christian Atheists," rejecting God and accepting Jesus. Their opponents exclaimed that this is like saying; "There is no God and Jesus is the chief prophet."

Second, this denial of God is combined with a positive affirmation of the individual and this world. One's first concern is the world in which one lives and dies. In this temporal realm one has to find and affirm one's faith and hope. One has to become "worldly" by involving oneself fully in this earthly existence and not fall back on some transcendent power to whom one can turn for help. The death-of-God theologians argue that the scientific and historical categories of reality are the only useful ones. All phases of the individual's thinking and experience have to be secularized including his or her religious and theological views. Yet this also means confidence in solving the problems of the world if one is to follow Jesus. The stress is on service rather than belief. This faith is "the secular meaning of the gospel."

There are some important differences between classical Protestant liberalism and the death-of-God theology. The former accepts the basic affirmations of the Christian gospel and tries to make these teachings palatable to the twentieth-century believer. The latter no longer can accept these Christian truths, for such ideas seem alien to the contemporary seeker. The earlier theology never questions the existence of God, but only whether God's presence can be better interpreted to the modern world. This later school is a movement within the church itself which denies God's existence. It represents the internalization of radical doubt within the church. Whereas the earlier movement assumed that the individual is ultimately dependent on God as creator, this new school contends that the individual must take full responsibility and have dominion over creation. Thus, despite the fact that both represent attempts to base theology on human experience, there remain important differences between Protestant liberalism and the death-of-God theology.

Four death-of-God theologians were prominent in the 1960s: William Hamilton, Paul van Buren, Thomas Altizer, and Richard Rubenstein. Each one approached the problem from a different perspective. William Hamilton's pivotal book, *The New Essence of Christianity* (1961), suggests a new view of God more appropriate to the contemporary world view. He contends that the problem of suffering has become for many Christians an insuperable obstacle to belief in the traditional loving, powerful God. He describes a growing sense of God's absence from human affairs.

> We wonder if God himself is not absent. When we speak of the death of God, we speak not only of the death of the idols or the falsely objectivized Being in the sky; we speak, as well, of the death in us of any power to affirm any of the traditional images of God.[13]

Hamilton's article entitled "Thursday's Child" which appeared in *Theology Today* in 1964 provides an elaboration of his theological views. In this article he declares that the theologian in America today is a person without faith who no longer believes in God, doesn't go to church, and doesn't write books on systematic theology. Indeed, the theologian is alienated from the Bible as well as God and the church. For Hamilton, God is no longer knowable in human experience. Hamilton elaborates, insisting that today's theologian cannot take seriously preaching, worship, prayer, ordination, and the sacraments. What, then, is left over for the theologian to affirm? For Hamilton, the turning away from God leads to an even more important turning toward the world and especially toward the man Jesus. Jesus represents "a place to be, a standpoint." The one who accepts Jesus accepts the world. But why Jesus rather than someone else? Hamilton answers:

> Jesus is the one to whom I stand, the one whose way with others is also to be my way because there is something there, in his words, his life, his way with others, his death, that I do not find elsewhere. I am drawn, and I have given my allegiance.[14]

But still, why Jesus? Is this not an arbitrary choice? Hamilton responds:

> I think I accept "arbitrary" as an adequate, if partial, description of the choice. It is arbitrary in that there are no inherent grounds in the object of that choice that compel my response. . . . Jesus is in the world in such a way that he *readies* me for whatever beliefs and actions and forms of self-discipline I may be obligated to take on. Not the "only," not the "best," but the one, nonetheless.[15]

Paul van Buren affirms the death of God by way of the analysis of language. Language about God is no longer meaningful since its claims are neither verifiable nor falsifiable. A statement of fact is one that makes some observable difference. But the existence of God has no empirical facts to support it. To quote him, "Today we cannot even understand the Nietzschean cry that "God is dead," for if it were so, how could we know? No, the problem now is that the *word* "God" is dead." [16] God-talk is meaningless. The term "God" is utterly incoherent. What does this imply about Christianity? Van Buren answers:

> I am trying to raise a more important issue: whether or not Christianity is fundamentally about God or about man. . . . I am trying to argue that it (Christianity) *is* fundamentally about man, that its language about God is one way . . . of saying what it is Christianity wants to say about man and human life and human history.[17]

Thus, the Christian faith must be about humanity and not about God. Fortunately, however, Christians are not lost, for they still have Jesus, the one who as a free man directs others to be free. The New Testament proclaims Jesus as a free man whose freedom becomes contagious.[18] This is the secular meaning of the gospel: an immanent Jesus without a transcendent God.

Thomas Altizer has a different slant. For him, the death of God occurred at the time of the coming of Jesus, a kind of mystical orgasm in which transcendence empties into immanence:

> The incarnation is only true and actually real if it effects the death of the original sacred, the death of God himself. . . . What is new in the Christian name of Jesus is the epiphany of the totality of the sacred in the contingency of a particular moment of time: in this name the sacred appears and is real only to the extent that it becomes actual and realized in history.[19]

Thus, for Altizer, God as transcendent has died, but God as immanent has been born again in the incarnation of Christ. God nullifies divine otherness in order that God might affirm human here-and-nowness. The Christian can proclaim the glad tidings that God is dead. This is the good news of the gospel. The death of God has occurred in a particular historical event, the Incarnation. The death is a *kenotic* (emptying) process. Its result is that God is Jesus, not vice versa. The Incarnation is only true if we accept the death of God:

The radical Christian proclaims that God has actually died in Christ, that this death is both a historical and a cosmic event, and as such, it is a final and irrevocable event, which cannot be reversed by a subsequent religious or cosmic movement.[20]

For the Jewish theologian Richard Rubenstein, the death of God hinges on the problem of evil. The death of six-million Jews in Germany during the Second World War makes it impossible to believe any longer in a loving God. Rubenstein writes:

When I say we live in the time of the death of God, I mean that the thread uniting God and man, heaven and earth, has been broken. We stand in a cold, silent, unfeeling cosmos, unaided by any purposeful power beyond our own resources. After Auschwitz, what else can a Jew say about God?[21]

What, then, of religion? All that we can do is to return to the gods of nature—of the rites of passage of birth, marriage, family, and death. We need our rituals of meaning to sustain us, but such meanings are human-centered and human-created. "Judaism is the way in which we share the decisive times and crises of life through the traditions of our inherited community."[22] But as far as the God of Abraham, Isaac, and Jacob is concerned, that God is dead. Omnipotent Nothingness is the Lord of all creation.[23]

By the end of the 1960s the death-of-God theology had virtually vanished, its fleeting popularity due in large part to exaggerations of the public press which precipitated both its dramatic rise and rapid fall. These theologians had either greatly modified their own positions or had stopped doing theology. The weakness of a death-of-God theology had become apparent, for it amounted to an almost complete capitulation to the narrow and arbitrary concerns of the modern world. It tended to accept uncritically the notion that secularization is a good thing, a weakness not unlike the liberalism of an earlier period which sought above all an accommodation with the modern scientific world view. The death-of-God theologians failed to heed the warning of the philosopher George Santayana that he who becomes married to the spirit of the times is destined to become a widower in the next generation. The death-of-God theologians were right in opposing the rigid dualism inherent in neo-orthodoxy and its arbitrary acceptance of revelation claims. But although it may be hard to conceive of the reality of God in our day, it is even more difficult to comprehend a world without God. This temporal realm must be affirmed, but have we become prisoners to secularism? What is so final about the here and now? Is humankind part of a deeper order of reality and is this reality accessible to human experience? And why this uncritical emphasis on Jesus as the pattern for living? Can we really know the historical Jesus, and even if we can, what makes the figure of Jesus unique? If we still insist on keeping Jesus as our model for living, is not part of that Jesus-model faith in God? What happens to prayer and worship, which were such vital dimensions of the religion of Jesus? Are these mere games that people play or are they legitimate aspects of the Jesus model? When we seek to be "relevant," we must ask: relevant to what, to whom, and for what purpose?

One of the most acclaimed books of the 1960s was Harvey Cox's *The Secular City* (1965). Here Cox suggests that the process of secularization has liberated the individual from the old supernatural images, and one is therefore free to create one's own secular myths which will affirm a new mood of living consistent with the present technological world. Cox's book is largely an analysis of the twin trends of the demise of traditional religion and the growth of urban civilization. He claims that the central features of the secular city, anonymity and mobility, present a new challenge to the urban believer. But Cox differs from the death-of-God theologians in seeing the hand of the transcendent God in this process. He concludes that secularization is a consequence of biblical faith which denies finality to all the old religious myths and institutions and enables humanity to discover and create new forms more in keeping with the present social and political urban order. Thus, secularization is in fact a maturing process for the individual which enables each person to assume responsibility for shaping the secular city in God's image. Cox seems to imply the old dualism affirmed by neo-orthodoxy, that biblical faith is God's search for the individual, while religion is the individual's search for God. Consequently, the replacing of the old with the new is God's way of showing the limitations of the old. Cox repudiates the death-of-God theologians for their failure to comprehend the biblical faith and their denial of the reality of God, but he agrees with them in praising the process of secularization and in finding a new confidence in human nature. We need to speak in a political way about God, conceive of God more as a verb than as a noun. "We speak of God politically whenever we give occasion to our neighbor to become the responsible, adult agent . . .

God expects him to be today.' '[24] By the end of the 1960s Cox had moderated his confidence in the glories of secularization and had moved on to a new emphasis, affirming the need for festivity and revelry in our over-secularized world and pointing to Christ as the number one harlequin (*The Feast of Fools*, 1969). Unlike the death-of-God proponents, Cox has remained an influential theologian primarily because of his willingness to shift with the changing theological currents.

Harvey Cox and the death-of-God theologians, although differing in significant respects, had tended to glorify secularism and to accept it as a *fait accompli*. But when secularism itself becomes a religion, its failures and weakness are apparent. For the basic questions of life still remain: what is the nature of ultimate reality? Is there a God? Does life have intrinsic meaning? It is as difficult to avoid these questions as it is to answer them. An adequate answer for today would acknowledge the secular world, but would also judge and transcend it.

Another theological trend that came to prominence in the middle and late sixties which proved to be an important contrast to the death-of-God phenomenon was the "theology of hope." These theologians, best represented by German theologians Jürgen Moltmann and Wolfhart Pannenberg, stress the eschatological dimension of history, understanding history as open to new possibilities, with God as the promise of ultimate fulfillment. To quote Moltmann:

> God is not somewhere in the Beyond, but he is coming and as the coming One he is present. He promises a new world of all-embracing life, of righteousness and truth, and with this promise he calls this world in question—not because to the eye of hope it is as nothing, but because to the eye of hope it is not yet what it has the prospect of being.[25]

These theologians underscore the social dimension of the historical process, viewing salvation as necessitating radical political and social change. God's revelation is made through political activity that is on the side of human liberation and social justice. God is not so much "above," "beyond," or "within," as God is the "power of the future" pulling humanity toward greater social fulfillment. According to Pannenberg, each person has the freedom to change, a freedom founded not "in being that already exists, but only in a reality which reveals to freedom its future, the coming God." [26] The theology of hope has remained largely a European phenomenon and its influence in

America has been mostly as a catalyst for political theologies. In particular, as we shall observe later, it has acted as a stimulus for some South American liberation theologians and a few North American black theologians. Unlike process theology it has never caught on as a movement in its own right; but unlike the death-of-God theology its influence on subsequent thinking has been deep and lasting.

An individual, difficult to fit into any of the above categories, who made a major impact on theological thinking in the 1960s, is Thomas Merton (1915–1968). A convert to Catholicism in his early years, Merton spent twenty-seven years at the Gethsemane monastery in Kentucky where he wrote extensively. His most famous book, *The Seven Storey Mountain* (1948), a bestseller in the 1950s and 1960s, tells the story of his constant struggle for solitude. In the 1960s he became involved in the vital social issues of the day. This was followed by his growing appreciation for Eastern mysticism. At the time of his unfortunate accidental death, Merton was visiting Thailand, expressing the need for an openness to other religions. Although he remained a steadfast Christian—Christianity, he said, was simply his language—he discerned, particularly in Taoism and Zen Buddhism, a depth of holiness which he insisted strengthened his own Christian mysticism. Had he lived into the 1970s and 1980s, Thomas Merton undoubtedly would have contributed enormously to interreligious dialogue and understanding.

Peter Berger's *A Rumor of Angels*, a little book published in 1969, further illustrates the demise of the death-of-God theology and suggests a new direction for theological thinking. Berger chastises the death-of-God theologians for their complete capitulation to the secular. He criticizes Cox for his glorification of the secular city, commenting, "Right now very few people in America are in a mood to celebrate much of anything in their city." [2] Berger contends that it is possible to see within the secular realm what he calls "signals of transcendence," signs of a deeper order of reality, that is, the supernatural. Instead of reducing theology to anthropology as the secular theologians had done, Berger reverses the process. He cites four factors in the secular order that point to the supernatural: 1) the human propensity for order which assumes a larger trusting destiny; 2) the argument from play which points from time to eternity; 3) the argument from hope which points toward a greater vindication and fulfillment; and 4) the argument from humor which helps the human spirit to be released from imprisonment in the here-and-now. Berger argues for an attitude of openness to larger dimensions of human experiences.

Probably the most cogent and thorough critique of the theologies of the 1960s is Langdon Gilkey's *Naming the Whirlwind: The Renewal of God-Language* (1969). Gilkey analyzes thoroughly the theological ferment and presuppositions of the 1960s and meets the theologians on their own terms. He correctly understands the real significance of the secular theologians in expressing the dominant mood of the times. But he also believes, as does Berger, that there is a hidden dimension of ultimacy in secular experience which he proceeds to delineate. "We wish only to show that a dimension of ultimacy does appear in our ordinary life and thus does give meaning to, and in fact provides the necessity for, religious symbols." [28] For Gilkey, secular individuals *as they live their lives* are more religious than they think they are. The power of love and meaning, and the freedom inherent in an open future, are essential ingredients pointing toward a transcendent totality, and the evidence for the existence of God emerges from the mysteries, wonders, and ambiguities of ordinary human life.

> The beginning of faith then appears in the awareness of the sacred in the profane, of joy and wonder in the midst of insecurity, of meaning and truth in the midst of the meaninglessness, and of life in the face of death, and it culminates with our understanding and affirmation of their ultimate unity in God.[29]

The secularism of the sixties had a powerful impact on theology. But by the end of that decade it was evident that those theologians who had capitulated to that spirit either were no longer taken seriously or had themselves moved on to other interests. As the mood of the country shifted from action to introspection, from liberalism to conservatism, theological interests reflected a similar though ambivalent change. On the one hand, some theologians confined their efforts primarily to one area of social change. If the Vietnam war and the rise of black consciousness could become focal points for a new kind of theology, this raised the possibility of other issue-oriented ideologies based on economic exploitation and sexism. The result was the splintering of theology so evident in the 1970s. On the other hand, some theologians, following the conservative introspective mood, opted for a more traditional evangelical faith that was reflected in a spiritual turning-within so typical of the ''turning to the East'' phenomenon and charismatic revival of the 1970s. It is to these developments that we now turn.

3

Black Theology

In one sense "black theology" is not a new phenomenon. Black people have always adapted the Christian faith to their own situation. Benjamin Mays' book *The Negro's God as Reflected in His Literature* (1938) traces the notion of God in black writings from the poem of Jupiter Hammon in 1761—"An Evening Thought: Salvation by Christ"— through the black spirituals, to the 1930s, and concludes that there are three abiding themes in this literature.

1. There is continuous insistence upon the view that God is no respecter of person; that from one blood, He created all mankind. The Negro will not accept the idea of a partial God.

2. The idea seems to persist that somehow things will work out to the advantage of the Negro—our cause is just; God is just; God is on the side of the right. This being true, the Negro cannot lose. The Negro insists upon having a God of justice and a God who is going to see to it that he wins through.

3. There is a constant note of doubt, frustration, protest, and cynicism, especially among the younger writers and particularly among the post-War writers. There are also expressions of atheism.[1]

In 1846 Frederick Douglass, affirming ambivalent feelings toward the Christianity exhibited by Jesus and practiced by his followers, exclaimed, "I hate the slaveholding, the mind-darkening, the soul-destroying religion that exists in America. Loving the one I must hate the other; holding to one I must reject the other."[2] In 1894 Henry McNeal Turner declared that "God is a Negro." Marcus Garvey (1887–1940), a forerunner of the Black Muslim and other black protest movements in this country, advocated a black God and black Jesus. Wherever and whenever black people have taken seriously Chris-

41

tianity's demands for righteousness and justice they have understood that God must be on the side of the oppressed. Black religion and the dignity of black people is not a new manifesto. Benjamin Mays writes in his autobiography, *Born to Rebel* (1971):

> Although I can appreciate the current emphasis on blackness, I am mighty glad I didn't have to wait seventy years for someone in the late 1960s to teach me to appreciate what I am—black![3]

However, it was not until the middle 1960s that the civil rights movement and the revolution of rising expectations led to a concerted effort by black theologians to develop and articulate a comprehensive view of the Christian gospel specifically for black people. In the early 1960s writings began to appear which anticipated the need for such a development. More than any other person, Martin Luther King, as a writer and activist, became a catalyst in the development of black theology. His brilliant "Letter from Birmingham Jail" (1963) focused on the plight of black people insisting that human progress is never inevitable, but is achieved only through divine and human partnership.[4] A year later Malcolm X published his autobiography. Malcolm became the most charismatic leader of the black revolution. Indeed, he more than any other gave the clarion call for black power. William Grier and Price Cobbs, the authors of *Black Rage* (1968), declare:

> History may show that of all the men who lived during our fateful century none illustrated the breadth or the grand potential of man so magnificently as did Malcolm X. If, in future chronicles, America is regarded as the major nation of our day, and the rise of darker people from bondage as the major event, then no figure has appeared thus far who captures the spirit of our times as does Malcolm.[5]

In his widely read *Black Religion* (1964) Joseph Washington undertakes a critical evaluation of black religion in America and condemns it for remaining outside of the mainstream of classical Christianity. The hallmark of religion among blacks, he maintains, has been emotionalism and other-worldliness, with the result that black churches had no theological underpinnings. The solution for black Christians is for them to close their own houses of worship and be accepted as full-fledged members in the white Christian churches. Only then will blacks become theologically sophisticated. By 1967, however,

Washington had drastically changed his position and argues in *The Politics of God* that the black churches should mobilize their own political power to achieve their own goals and should not be dependent on or assimilated into the white churches. He suggests that the black ministers and churches should form their own political power bases to effect social change, and that the destiny of blacks is to be a "suffering servant people." Washington condemns Martin Luther King's non-violent techniques for simply "calling men to bleed in social action for the purposes of a hamburger"[6] and insists that

> the task of the Negro is not to change the minds and hearts of dominant whites. The task is to change their world. . . . This is not only black politics, it is good politics, it is the demand of the Kingdom of God—the rudimentary principles and practices of the politics of God.[7]

One can surmise two reasons for his changing views. First, his earlier book *Black Religion* advocating black capitulation to white churches and failing to discern a theological uniqueness to black religion was not well received by the black community. Moreover, the mood of black people in the middle 1960s had changed to a much more radical and separatist position typified by the phrase "black power," a phrase popularized by Stokely Carmichael in 1966. That year a group of black clergymen drafted a statement in support of black power, a document which became the platform for the National Committee of Black Churchmen. The authors of *Black Rage* articulate the underlying concerns of black power when they write:

> People bear all they can and, if required, bear even more. But if they are black in present-day America they have been asked to shoulder too much. They have had all they can stand. They will be harried no more. Turning from their tormentors, they are filled with rage.[8]

Thus by 1966 it became incumbent for black theologians to articulate a theology in harmony with the new consciousness of black power.

In anticipation of this need Albert Cleage, a black minister in Detroit, published *The Black Messiah* (1968) portraying Jesus as a revolutionary black leader whose purpose is to free black people from oppression. Cleage exhorts his own people:

> We issue a call to all black churches. Put down this white Jesus who has been tearing you to pieces. Forget your white God. Remember that we are

worshipping a Black Jesus who was a Black Messiah. Certainly God must be black if he created us in his own image.[9]

This same black militancy was expressed a year later in the Black Manifesto. On 4 May 1969 James Forman interrupted a Sunday morning worship service at Riverside Church in New York City and issued a statement to the white churches and synagogues and all other racist institutions in the United States demanding five hundred million dollars—"fifteen dollars per nigger"—from these organizations as reparations for the mistreatment of the black people by "the most vicious, racist system in the world."[10] The Black Manifesto had been the product of a conference on black economic development held a month earlier in Detroit. This document probably caused more turmoil in the life of the churches than any event since the assassination of Martin Luther King in 1967, for it revealed the magnitude of the bitterness of black people toward the white people and their churches.

Until 1969, however, there had been no over-all coherent theological interpretation of what black power meant for black religious people. This changed with the appearance of *Black Theology and Black Power* by James Cone. The thesis of Cone's book is that "Black Power, even in its most radical expression, is not the antitheses of Christianity. . . . It is, rather, Christ's central message to twentieth-century America."[11] Black power means "complete emancipation of black people from white oppression by whatever means black people deem necessary."[12] Cone proceeds to articulate a black theology consistent with the claims and rhetoric of black power. The only reason for having a black theology is to utilize the Christian faith as a means of liberating black people from white oppression. Christ is involved in supporting black power. He is behind the black revolution. "Whether whites want to hear it or not, *Christ is black, baby*, with all of the features which are so detestable to white society."[13] To consider Christ as nonblack in our time would, says Cone, be as wrong as to consider him as non-Jewish in the first century. Cone criticizes the death-of-God theology as "child's play," as the epitome of human pride in ignoring the reality of God and succumbing to secular society. He finds confirmation of his own views in Jürgen Moltmann's theology of hope, especially in Moltmann's contention that God is fighting against suffering and oppression. But Cone's main concern is to develop views of God, Christ, humanity, and the Church that would support the liberation of black people from their white oppressors. The task of black theology is

to analyze the black man's condition in the light of God's revelation in Jesus Christ with the purpose of creating a new understanding of black dignity among black people, and providing the necessary soul in that people, to destroy white racism.[14]

Cone's rhetoric is strident in his attempt to appeal to the proponents of black power. His language is not likely to endear him to his white contemporaries. He implies that blacks will have nothing to do with whites and he seems to condone violence as sometimes essential to secure the black person's rights. It is not until the very end of his book that he explains:

Being black in America has very little to do with skin color. To be black means that your heart, your soul, your mind, and your body are where the dispossessed are. . . . Being reconciled to God does not mean that one's skin is physically black. It essentially depends on the color of your heart, soul, and mind.[15]

In his next book, *A Black Theology of Liberation* (1970), Cone elaborates upon the theme of blackness as an ontological symbol standing for oppression. However, this point continues to be lost in the vehemence of his anti-white rhetoric.

To be black is to be committed to destroying everything this country loves and adores.[16]

The goal of Black Theology is the destruction of everything *white* so that black people can be alienated from alien gods.[17]

Black theology will accept only a love of God which participates in the destruction of the white enemy.[18]

Black and White Power Subreption (1969), Joseph Washington's third book, provides another militant interpretation of the black power movement. He maintains that black power's roots are to be found in the social and religious experience of black Americans. He speaks with approval of Albert Cleage and James Cone and insists, "It is the central spirit of Black Power which declares that the only creative source for blacks is in and through violent encounter with whites."[19] Washington concludes, "There is a tough-minded side of me which cannot see any real basis for a new society called for by Black Power apart from a racial war to this end.''[20] The militant views of Cone and Washington made it difficult, if not impossible, for nonblack theologians to enter into dialogue with them. Thus the responsibility for providing critiques and further clarification of black theology fell to other black theologians.

Deotis Roberts presents a less strident approach in his book *Liberation and Reconciliation: A Black Theology* (1971). He recognizes the importance of black theology in enabling black people to affirm their God-given humanity. But he does not interpret this need univocally and, therefore, cannot think of Christ as being black in any literal sense. He criticizes Albert Cleage's concept of a literal black messiah. For Roberts, a universal Christ must be personal and relevant to people of all races. A black Christ would be as parochial as a yellow or white Christ. He also disapproves of James Cone's capitulation to the narrow separatism of black power. Roberts maintains:

> While Cone confesses an indifference to whites, *I care.* . . . It is my desire to speak to blacks and whites *separately*, but in the long run it is hoped that real intercommunication between blacks and whites may result. . . . James Cone is on the fence between the Christian faith and the religion of Black Power. It will be necessary for Cone to decide presently where he will take his firm stand. The present writer takes his stand within the Christian theological circle.[21]

Thus, Roberts includes reconciliation between blacks and whites as an indispensable dimension of Christian liberation. For him, this does not mean integration, which he views as a strictly white goal. What we should seek, he declares, is a "constructive, deeply motivated, long-range, massive reorientation in black-white relations."[22] This cannot come through violence.

In his book *Black Awareness: A Theology of Hope* (1971), Major Jones sees in the theology of hope and especially in Jürgen Moltmann a solid justification for black theology, for it places the hope of black people squarely in a God who fights against racial oppression in the historical realities of this world. Contrary to Joseph Washington's denigration of the black preacher as lacking in theological sophistication, Jones contends that it was precisely the black slave preacher who kept alive the vision of hope. Jones, like Roberts, is wary of justifying violence and also of translating Christian categories into exclusively black ones. "Will the black man, with his black God, be a better man than the white man was with his white God?"[23] He, too, is critical of James Cone's separatism which suggests that God is only on the side of the blacks. Jones raises the possibility that the extremists among the black theologians are more interested in an ideology of revolution and less concerned with God's involvement in this struggle. For Jones, as for Roberts, the ultimate goal must be reconciliation among the races. Both blacks and whites must come together and fully accept and respect "a pluralism of ideologies, interests, aims and aspirations, and person-hood; and no one will for any purpose be denied opportunity to achieve, or be excluded from community."[24] Although Jones and Roberts are united in their criticism of Cone and Cleage, they differ in their assessment of the theology of hope. Jones, as we have noted, incorporates Moltmann's insights into his black theology. Roberts admits that the theology of hope has "a good psychological ring for a hopeless people"; however, he contends that it does not ring true to the black experience and is more germane to the Marxist Christian dialogue in Europe. Roberts writes:

> I have some personal reservations about the theology of hope. Any theological outlook requires some "indigenization" before it is suitable as a formulation of the Christian understanding of the black experience. . . . The theme of the "waiting God" is unacceptable for those who have been waiting so long—who are tired of waiting.[25]

Also published in 1971 was Columbus Salley and Roland Behm's *Your God is Too White*, another moderate approach to black theology. Salley and Behm insist that

> The white Jesus is dead. He was slain somewhere between Hiroshima or Nagasaki and the road to Selma, Alabama. And that Jesus will never be resurrected as the Christ. The book you are reading will tell you that he will remain forever entrapped amidst the images of pristinity which white middle-class America mistakes for purity.[26]

But they also have misgivings about the "black Jesus." They accuse Cleage and others of substituting one narrow ideology for another by defining Christianity solely on the basis of color.

It is clear that by 1971 vigorous debate had developed among the proponents of black theology, a debate that centered on the issue: is black theology exclusively an instrument for the liberation of black people from white oppression, or should it be an instrument of reconciliation among the races and between the oppressed and oppressor? Should black theology be solely concerned with its own particular "inner history," or should it build bridges with the universal "outer history" shared by all humankind? Hart Nelson's *The Black Church in America* (1971) provides a series of readings by black thinkers interpreting both the past and present state of affairs in black religion. One is struck by the plurality of positions represented in this work. Clearly black theology can no longer be considered a monolith.

Albert Cleage reaffirms his own particularistic commitment to his earlier concept of the black messiah in his later book *Black Christian Nationalism: New Directions for the Black Church* (1972). He finds in the exodus of Moses and his people from Egypt to create a Black Nation a paradigm for the black people of today seeking to establish a new Promised Land.

> Believing that nothing is more sacred than the liberation of Black people, we are a revolutionary Pan-African movement dedicated to the building of a heaven on earth in the here and now for all Black people everywhere.[27]

Cleage criticizes the black leaders of his time—Ralph Abernathy, Andrew Young, and Jessie Jackson—for their commitment to integration and thereby the creation of a nonpeople. For Cleage, white people are the enemy; indeed "the white man is a beast" and "white Christianity is a bastard religion without a Messiah and without a God."[28] According to Cleage, black people need to create a "nation within a nation" and to require every person joining this Black Christian Nationalist Movement to undergo a one-year training program before attaining full membership. Each member would make the following covenant with one another.

> Declaring ourselves to be God's Chosen People, created in His image, the living of the lost Black Nation, Israel, we come together as brothers and sisters in the Black Christian Nationalist Movement. We are disciples of the Black Messiah, Jesus of Nazareth, who by his life, and by his death upon the cross, teaches us that nothing is more sacred than the liberation of Black people.
>
> We covenant together, and pledge our total commitment to the task of

rebuilding a Black Nation with power, here on earth. We will do whatever is necessary to achieve self-determination for Black people. We will fight the injustice, oppression, and exploitation of all Black People. As members of the Black Nation, we are bound together in an inseparable sacred brotherhood. To the service of this sacred brotherhood, we pledge our lives.[29]

Joseph Washington's *Black Sects and Cults* (1972) provides a response to Cleage's proposal. Although Washington and Cleage are in basic agreement that black theology and a black Jesus are exclusively for black people, Washington insists that Cleage does not realize the significance of the black cult. Washington believes that there is a "common ethnic ethic"[30] among black people which should be the basis of black religion, a basis which Washington believes that Cleage has failed to articulate. Washington affirms that black religion combines the suffering of the African heritage with the hope of Christian faith. The indifference of the established white churches to the spirtual needs of the black people has made it imperative for the black people to shape their own faith on the American scene, a movement which has resulted in the emergence of distinctive black sects and cults. Thus, the purpose of black theology is not to articulate a Christian theology in relation to racism and the black experience—as James Cone and Deotis Roberts are trying to do—but, rather, to work out the relationship between black people in sects and cults and the American experience.

Meanwhile, with the publication of *Black Religion and Black Radicalism* (1972), Gayraud Wilmore enters the black theological debate. In his book he seeks to analyze the growth of black religion from the early period of slavery in America to the latest theological developments related to the black power movement. He contends that, although historically black American religion has been a basically conservative evangelical movement, undergirding it is a distinctive black religious experience with roots in its African past, which has, nevertheless, been profoundly affected by the stigma of oppression and slavery. Wilmore claims that there remained in the unconscious memory of the slave a residue of the African past which arose time and time again to give him hope. Wilmore advocates increasing communication between American and African religious leaders to create a new black theology that will "bind black people together, inside and outside of churches, in the solidarity of a new faith in God and humanity.[31] Thus we might say that James Cone seeks to relate black theology to black power; Joseph Washington, black theology to the black sects and cults of the American scene; and Gayraud Wilmore, black theology to the black religious experience that includes both African and American dimensions. In so doing, all three theologians are basically confining themselves to the treatment of the particularistic "inner history" of black people.

The intramural critique of black theology continued with the publication of William Jones' *Is God a White Racist? A Preamble to Black Theology* (1973). He criticizes all of the black theologians for not taking seriously the problem of evil. He cannot reconcile the inordinate suffering of black people with the traditional affirmations of God's goodness and sovereignty over history. God is a white racist if God permits the black people to suffer so at the hands of white people. William Jones uses the oppression of black people as his reason for denying God's existence in the same way that Richard Rubenstein makes Auschwitz his reason for disbelief. He introduces the concept of "humanocentric theism" which gives to human beings responsibility and power heretofore reserved for God.[32] Despite James Cone's attempted response,[33] an adequate answer to William Jones's sharp challenge to the other black theologians on the issue of theodicy has yet to appear.

Other black theologians have continued to stress the universal dimension as imperative for black theology. In his book *Christian Faith in Black and White* (1973), Warner Traynham sounds a universal note in declaring that black theology "can no longer ignore the other theologies of liberation that are arising. While its perspective and experience are different, yet, if truth is a whole, they must be related."[34] Deotis Roberts' *A Black Political Theology* (1974) provides another kind of thoroughgoing critique of the black theologies produced by his colleagues. Here he develops further the theme of his earlier work that liberation and reconciliation go hand in hand.

> The only Christian way in race relations is a liberating experience of reconciliation for the white oppressor as well as the black oppressed. That is what a black theology is all about, and its message is to the whole church of Christ.[35]

He criticizes most of the theological trends of the 1960s for being too European and more interested in logical precision than social change. He attacks the Harvey Cox who moved gleefully from "the secular city" to "the feast of fools" embracing "holy hippies" almost as the very chosen of God (who) now ponder the meaning of this new retreat from social evils.[36]

Again, he rejects Jürgen Moltmann's theology of hope, portraying it as "highly theoretical, ivory-tower pursuits indulged in by those far removed by race and space from the fray."[37] He objects to Albert Cleage's Jesus "who is black, alive, and well" and dismisses James Cone's view of Christ as evidence of a "Barthian hangup"[38] and a failure to take seriously the African roots of black religion. But Roberts does see real promise in South American liberation theology, with its identification with the oppressed peoples. He maintains that black and liberation theologies share a common political basis in that they focus attention on the political, economic, and social dimensions of religion.

Major Jones's second book, *Christian Ethics for Black Theology: The Politics of Liberation* (1974), also leans toward a move away from racial particularism and contemporary concerns, and toward universality, this time in the form of timeless eternal values which transcend color boundaries. He examines the roots of black Christian ethics in the Old and New Testaments and contends that God as "Holy Being" means that God is not just black, as James Cone suggests; for if God is not the God of everyone, God is the God of no one. He criticizes Cone and Albert Cleage for too much dependence on the black power movement which has encouraged a sense of hatred which stifles the human spirit. Jones pleads for an ethic of hope, proposing that his book "is offered to remind us all, black and white, that the future may well belong to those who hope for the simple reason that they are the only people who have something to live for." [39]

Similarly the black poet Julius Lester in an article "Be Ye Therefore Perfect" sharply criticizes the narrow "God is black" and "white racist" slogans of James Cone, William Jones, and others. Lester insists:

Black theologians are not breaking with tradition, but merely joining it. What is there to distinguish them from the priests of the eleventh century, who claimed that God wanted Europe to go forth on a Crusade and cut the throats of the infidels. . . . Whenever we become absolutists about God and the way He moves in history we perpetrate violence. . . . Black theology is shameful because its spokesmen want us to believe that blacks are without sin. . . . If black theology is a good example of what comes out of seminaries, a lot of folks just might be better off back in the cotton fields.[40]

James Cone's *God of the Oppressed* (1975) indicates the relevance of black theology to his own faith as it was shaped by the black community. He questions the importance of the African religious tradition to black people in America. His thesis is that one's own personal social matrix determines both the form and content of one's own faith, that there can be no black theology which does not take the black experience as a source for its starting point.[41] Thus white theologians necessarily have a different mind set and can never appreciate black theology. How could such theologians get inside of the experience of slavery? White theologians have been spectators rather than victims. Their views of God and Christ have been shaped by philosophy and not by human servitude. Christ is black both literally and symbolically. The "blackness of Christ" means that "God has not ever, no not ever, left the oppressed alone in the struggle.'"[42] White theologians will never understand this. James Cone criticizes Deotis Roberts for suggesting that black people should forget their servitude and seek reconciliation with their white oppressors. Such affiliation is impossible. Cone concludes:

> It is therefore black people's reconciliation with each other, in America, Africa, and the islands of the sea, that must be the black theologians' primary concern. For unless we can get together with our African brothers and sisters for the shaping of our future, then white capitalists in America and Europe will destroy us.[43]

Cecil Cone's *The Identity Crisis in Black Theology* (1975) represents the culmination of these initial attempts at self-criticism within black theology. Here Cone articulates the tensions undergirding the recent developments in black theology. What is the relationship of black theology to black power? Should black theologians be loyal primarily to the black religious experience or to the greater theological community of faith? Must black theology be constructed from the historical critical method intrinsic to Western theologians or should it above all reflect the experience of American blacks? Cecil Cone examines the views of Joseph Washington, James Cone, and Deotis Roberts to indicate the areas of disagreement which precipitated the identity crisis.

First, he notes that Joseph Washington has radically changed his views over the years. Whereas in *Black Religion* (1964) he pleads with white people to include blacks in their churches so that black people could "come of age" theologically, in *The Politics of God* (1967)

Washington contends that the hope for humankind is to be found in the black religious community. Cecil Cone accuses Washington of distorting the black religious tradition in stressing more of the implications of black power than the sovereign God.

> The problem here is Washington's use of the Black Power motif as primary in his analysis of black religion. In so doing, he is unable to deal with the fullness of the black religious experience. He has reduced the phenomenon to a social, economic, and political movement.[44]

Cecil Cone suggests that his brother James has been too uncritical of the black power movement. He maintains that James Cone's demand that the black church adopt the spirit of black power has been off the mark and that his very dependence on the politically based black power theme distorts his perspective of black experience. Cecil admits that James tries to rectify this narrow approach in his book *A Black Theology of Liberation* by expounding a systematic treatment of the Christian faith in the light of the black American experience. Nevertheless, Cecil Cone asserts, James's defense of the historical-critical method downgrades the importance of the black religious experience.

> [James] must make up his mind concerning his confessional commitment: Is it to the black religious experience or to the Black Power motif of liberation with a side-long glance at the black religious experience? As long as it is the latter, so long will he suffer an essential inconsistency.[45]

Likewise Cecil Cone criticizes Deotis Roberts' methodology for being centered more in the comprehensive field of theology than in the uniqueness of the black religious experience. While Roberts accuses James Cone of making blackness an exclusive symbol thus preventing intercommunication between blacks and whites, Cecil Cone faults Roberts for his espousal of universalism which "is really a guise for specific, Euro-American categories that are in themselves alien to black religious history." [46] Cecil Cone sees the source of the identity crisis for black theologians in their zealous uncritical "identification with the academic structure of white seminaries and with the Black Power motif of black radicals." [47] Cecil Cone affirms that if black theology is to interpret accurately the black religious experience

> it will become not so much a theology of and for black people but of and for the glorification of God. . . . Black Theology must come to terms not with black people as such, but with the God of black people, the One who

encountered the people in their concrete and peculiar circumstances and gave them "the imagination to think of a good reason to keep on keepin' on," and the power "to make the best of a bad situation." [48]

Since 1975 the identity crisis in black theology has intensified as black theologians have sought to clarify the relationship of black theology to the particularities of the black religious experience as well as the larger dimensions of a liberation theology outside the black community. Warner Traynham describes the dilemma in his *Black Theology Lecture Series* (1977): "Is Black Theology truly ethnic, or truly a liberation theology. . . . Is Black Theology one theological perspective among many? . . . Is it the only Christian theology?" [49] James Cone had contributed to the problem in his first book in 1969 (*Black Theology and Black Power*) by his ambiguous use of the term *black* both as a reference to the black community and as an ontological symbol not dependent on the color black. This ambiguity has remained in his writing. In 1975 he wrote:

> I also believe that Christian theology must be black theology. . . . To say that Christ is black, therefore, means that God has taken sides with oppressed blacks in their struggle to overthrow the white oppressors. . . . Indeed, if God is not black in himself, then Jesus lied.[50]

Here Cone appears to be making an exclusive connection between black theology, a black God, and black people. But by 1977 Cone had begun to abandon this narrow interpretation of Christian theology.

> I think that the time has come for black theologians and church people to move beyond a mere reaction to white racism in America and begin to extend our vision of a new socially constructed humanity in the whole inhabited world. We must be concerned with the quality of human life not only in the ghettoes of American cities but also in Africa, Asia, and Latin America. For humanity is whole, and cannot be isolated into racial and national groups. Indeed there will be no freedom for anyone until there is freedom for all. . . . Liberation knows no color bar. Unlike oppression that is often limited to color, the very nature of the gospel is universalism, that is, a liberation that embraces the whole of humanity.[51]

This statement suggests that Cone is moving to the right and closer to the views of Deotis Roberts and Major Jones who see reconciliation as a key factor in liberation.

Meanwhile black theologians in America are also trying to come to terms with their African religious tradition. Gayraud Wilmore and Deotis Roberts are especially interested in their African past. Henry Mitchell in his book *Black Belief: Folk Beliefs of Blacks in America and West Africa* (1975) makes the same point, suggesting that

> the folk religion of the masses of Blackamericans is clearly an adaptation of the African-traditional-religion base brought over by the various West Africans who were pressed into slavery. Black Religion today is quite properly understood to be profoundly Christian, but it is also still deeply influenced by its African roots.[52]

Warner Traynham insists, however, that black Americans are peculiarly American, that Africa may be in the American black person's future, but not the past. Clearly the relationship of American black theology to African black theology will be an important item on the agenda for black theologians. Allan Boesak, a black theologian in South America, has criticized American black theologians—especially James Cone—for absolutizing the black American experience.

> Cone's mistake is that he has taken black theology out of the framework of liberation theology, thereby making his own situation (being black in America) and his own movement (liberation from white racism) the ultimate criterion for *all theology*.[53]

Boesak develops this thesis in his book *Farewell To Innocence: A Social-Ethical Study of Black Theology and Black Power* (1976).

> While we acknowledge that the expressions of liberation theology are not identical, we must object very strongly against the total division (and contrast) some make between Black Theology in South Africa and Black Theology in the United States; between Black Theology and African Theology; between Black Theology and Latin American theology of liberation. As a matter of principle, we have therefore treated all these different expressions within the framework where they belong: the framework of the theology of liberation.[54]

Boesak asserts that racism is not the only demon, a point underscored by Warner Traynham, who notes that in Latin America, for example, racial distinctions are less significant than class divisions.

Future American black theologians must not only enter into dialogue with other black theologians in other parts of the world whose situations may be different from the black American experience, but also make contact with other liberation theologians—women, South American, American Indian, etc.—for whom oppression comes in different forms. A first encounter of this kind occurred in Detroit in 1975 when black, feminist, and South American liberation theologians met to discuss their different and common objectives. The lack of understanding at this conference is evident in Martin Garate's words. "Black theologians are suspicious that liberation theology is white theology; in the same way theologians in Latin America are suspicious that black theology is more American than black." [55]

The biggest challenge facing some black American theologians is to try to break out of their introverted mentality. These black theologians seem primarily to be talking to and influencing one another, with little or no concern for the "outer history" that all people share. There is little evidence that a parochial black theology has had much impact even on the black churches. Indeed, Peter Paris' book *Black Leaders in Conflict* (1978) indicates that the black leaders themselves disagree with one another, not only on theology, but on social issues. Paris notes that Joseph H. Jackson presents a devastating criticism of James Cone, maintaining that he "not only polarizes blacks and whites in this country, but he freezes that polarization and leaves little or no latitude for future harmony to be achieved." [56] Jackson suggests the direction of black theology in the future, affirming that

> Any theologian, be he black or white, that limits the redemptive effort of Jesus Christ to any race, to any color, to any nationality, or any rank or group in society denies and negates the positive principles of redemption. [56]

An indication of a new development in this area is the book *Black Theology II: Essays on the Formation and Outreach of Contemporary Black Theology* (1978). The authors of these eleven essays—includng black, white, and feminist thinkers—claim that what they call Black Theology I has made its significant contribution and that the time has come for new directions.

> Urgent among the concerns of this facet of Black Theology II is the need to broaden the dialogical strength of black theological discourse. On the one hand, this demands that black theologians be in spirited dialogue among themselves and with all segments of the black church. On the other hand, this need for communicative redirection urges that black theologians profit from the dialogue into which many white theologians are willing to enter

. . . Also, it is felicitous for black theology to reach out to embrace other vanguards of the human liberation movement.[58]

In similar fashion Clyde Holbrook declares that

dialogue between white and black theology not only remains a possibility, but is imperative. . . . If the word *racist* has any identifiable meaning left in it, black theology is an example of racist thinking. It takes as a primary category not suffering and oppression as such, but blackness.[59]

And black theologian Deotis Roberts, in an accusation reminiscent of what black theologians have said about their white counterparts, declares:

The leadership of the scholars seems to be gravitating toward those black professors who have plush professorships in Ivy League universities or ranking theological seminaries that are predominantly white in outlook and program. Could it be that while black scholars talk black, they really prize the fact that the white world has cast the mantle of respectability on them? . . . If this trend continues, black theology will not be church theology—it will be ivory-tower theology, and its spokesmen will have joined the bandwagon of most American and European theologians who are addicted to an arid theological scholasticism that is dry bones for faith.[60]

Another important recent book is *African Theology En Route* (1979), a selection of articles emanating from the Pan-African Conference of Third World Theologians held in Ghana in December 1977. This conference included primarily black theologians from the Third World who stated:

We believe that African theology must be understood in the context of African life and culture and the creative attempt of African peoples to shape a new future that is different from the colonial past and the neo-colonial present. The African situation requires a new theological methodology that is different from the approaches of the dominant theologies of the West. African theology must reject, therefore, the prefabricated ideas of North Atlantic theology by defining itself according to the struggles of the people in their resistance against the structures of domination. Our task as theologians is to create a theology that arises from and is accountable to African people.[61]

What is particularly significant about this conference is that American black theologian James Cone now finds himself on the defensive in his encounter with Third World black theologians. Cone, who had long insisted that "whites can never understand blacks," is now told that North American blacks can never understand Third World blacks, that the interest in one another can be only peripheral.[62] In a reversal of roles, Cone objects to this view which eliminates black American theologians from having a role in the development of black African theology. "Black and African theologies are not as different as has been suggested and their common concerns require a dialogue that is important to both." [62]

Finally, Gayraud Wilmore and James Cone have edited *Black Theology: A Documentary History, 1969–1979,* a collection focused primarily on politics and social action. Many black theologians—such as Deotis Roberts, William R. Jones, Joseph Washington, Major Jones, and Cecil Cone—are not included, on the grounds that they are too "academic" and "professional." The strength of this book lies in its inclusion of about twenty-five significant statements by groups of black churchmen during this period, sections on black women and the relationship between black theology and third world theologies, and a comprehensive annotated bibliography. Its weakness is that it is in large part a defense of the views of the editors. Gayraud Wilmore states in the general introduction that, "In contrast to most of White theological writing, a strong personal note runs through what Cone and I have written here. We have, in a sense, "testified." [64] Eleven of the individually authored essays were written by Cone, including several introductions to sections of the book which gave him the opportunity to rebut certain of the essays. The epilogue gives Cone's interpretation the last word on the contemporary debate among black theologians.

It seems clear that black theology must come to terms with a wider liberation theology. An increasingly vocal element among black theologians no longer finds it satisfactory to restrict themselves to "thinking black." Blackness has become as varied and ambiguous a term as whiteness. The time has come for black theologians to make common cause with thinkers of whatever race, sex, color, or nationality who seek for liberation from human servitude of all kinds and who seek to serve the God who abhors all forms of oppression.

4

South American Liberation Theology

Black theology did not arise spontaneously in the late 1960s; instead it traces its roots to African and early American sources. Similarly, South American "liberation theology" points to its origins in earlier manifestations of the Christian missionary impulse on that continent; however, liberation theology is at least as much a reaction *against* Christian mission as an affirmation of it. The missionaries more often than not sided with the oligarchies. While present-day liberation theologians can look back on the colonization process since Columbus "discovered" America in 1492 and insist that "the conquest of America was nothing more than oppression,"[1] it is still a fact that the missionaries, who began arriving in the sixteenth century, came because they believed, however imperfectly, that the Christian faith should be transmitted to all corners of the earth. Indeed, Enrique Dussel suggests that liberation theology had its antecedents in Bartolemé de las Casas, a courageous advocate of the rights of the Indians in the sixteenth century.[2] However, he was more the exception than the rule.

One must not downplay the historical domination of Latin America—socially, politically, economically, and religiously—by land-owning European capitalist overlords. In the early nineteenth century the struggle to achieve political freedom from Spain and Portugal led to the rise of nation-states and to a gradual shift from dependence on European powers to economic subservience to the United States. Political freedom did not mean real independence for the masses. Dependence, whether political or economic, remained the basic fact of life. The increasing trend toward industrialization which began in the 1930s only served to keep the masses suppressed.

The Social-Christian movement which emerged in Europe in the middle of the nineteenth century and which was encouraged by the Catholic Church at the end of that century under the leadership of Pope Leo XIII did not become a major force in Latin America until the 1950s. In 1959 the socialist revolution in Cuba succeeded, a sign of what could happen to the entire southern hemisphere. The stark reality of the situation in South America has been well described by historian Arthur Schlesinger, Sr.

> Here is a subcontinent where one-eighth more people than the population of the United States subsist on less than one-eighth of our gross national product, where 5 per cent of the people receive a third of the income and 70 per cent live in abject poverty, and where in country after country the political and social structures are organized to keep things that way.[3]

It was not until the late 1960s that liberation theology emerged in South America as a self-conscious movement. The great catalyst for change in the earlier part of that decade was Vatican II, especially under the leadership of Pope John XXIII. In the words of Peter Wagner:

> When historians evaluate this period a century from now, it may well turn out that Pope John XXIII will have been judged to have had more influence on the Latin American continent than any other man in the twentieth century. Roman Catholicism will never be the same as a result of the council he called and the attitude he infused.[4]

Enrique Dussel suggests that another pivotal event occurred in 1964 when Dom Helder Camara, shortly after becoming a bishop in Brazil, delivered an address with these opening words:

> I am a native of northeast Brazil, speaking to other natives of that region, with my gaze focused on Brazil, Latin America, and the world. I speak as a human being, in fellowship with the frailty and sinfulness of all other human beings, as a Christian to other Christians, but with a heart open to all individuals, peoples, and ideologies; as a bishop of the Catholic Church who, like Christ, seeks to serve rather than be served. May my fraternal greetings be heard by all: Catholics and non-Catholics, believers and non-believers. Praised be Jesus Christ.[5]

Through his writings and witness Helder Camara has been a continuing advocate of the rights of the poor and in 1974 was awarded the People's Peace Prize, the alternative to the Nobel Prize.

Another important figure was Camilo Torres of Colombia, a priest who in the early 1960s renounced his comfortable university position to cast his lot and life with the poor, an act which eventually led to his assassination. When Torres left the priesthood, he made a statement which became a rallying statement for other radicals.

I have left the privileges and duties of the clergy, but I have not left the priesthood. I believe to have devoted myself to the revolution out of love for my neighbor. I will not say the Mass, but I will realize this love to my neighbor in the temporal, economic and social realms. When my neighbor has nothing against me, when I have realized the revolution, I will then say the Holy Mass again.[6]

The martyred Che Guevara, another priest-turned-radical reformer, has likewise become a hero for the social revolutionaries.

In 1966 the World Council of Churches Conference on Church and Society met in Geneva and for the first time heard from South American religious leaders about the new theological movements in their continent. Gonzalo Castillo Cardenas declared at this conference that it may be

necessary to take power away from the privileged minorities and give it to the poor majorities. . . . Revolution can be peaceful if the minorities do not resist violently. . . . Revolution is not only permitted, but it is obligatory for those Christians who see it as the only effective way of fulfilling love to one's neighbor.[7]

Richard Shaull, then a missionary in Brazil and now a professor at Princeton Seminary, declared at the same meeting:

This is what we most desperately need today: men liberated for creativity, participating in a community in which they are forced to die daily in order to create new ideas, new perspectives, new experiments, new institutions, new political possibilities. . . . It is essential now to develop, within institutions, small groups of people committed to constantly upsetting their stability, taking new initiatives and launching new experiments. . . . and willing to pay the price of such subversive acts which will not always be appreciated.[8]

The most important event by far for the emergence of a new theological outlook was the conference of Latin American bishops (CELAM II) which met in Medellin, Colombia in 1968. The theme of this meeting was "The Church in the Present-Day Transformation of Latin America in the Light of the Council," referring to the Second Vatican Council of the early 1960s. Here in sixteen different documents the Latin American bishops focused their concern on the plight of the poor, denouncing the capitalist monopolies and demanding that "it appears to be a time of zeal for full emancipation, of liberation from every form of servitude, of personal maturity and of collective integration."[9] The Medellin documents stress the point that people must be liberated in all their dimensions: social, personal, national, and that "Latin America will undertake its liberation at the cost of whatever sacrifice."[10]

What is South American liberation theology? Basically it is the effort to relate the teachings of the Christian faith to the lives of the poor and oppressed. Theology begins and ends with the downtrodden and their vision of life. What does the Christian faith have to say to and do for the millions of oppressed people who are caught in the chains of poverty? Theology is not right thinking about the nature of ultimate reality in order to convince the nonbeliever that God exists. Rather, theology is the explication of the condition of the oppressed in their misery for the purpose of alleviating their inhuman plight. Gustavo Gutiérrez, the leading exponent of this view of theology, puts it this way:

> In a continent like Latin America . . . the main challenge does not come from the nonbeliever but from the nonhuman—that is, the human being who is not recognized as such by the prevailing social order. These are the poor and exploited people, the ones who are systematically and legally despoiled of their being human, those who scarcely know what a human being might be. These nonhumans do not call into question our religious world so much as they call into question our *economic, social, political, and cultural world.* Their challenge impels us toward a revolutionary transformation of the very bases of what is now a dehumanizing society. The question, then, is no longer how we are to speak about God in a world come of age; it is rather how to proclaim him Father in a world that is not human and what the implications might be of telling nonhumans that they are children of God.[11]

The main features of liberation theology are to be found in this quotation from Gutiérrez. The purpose of this theology is to humanize the oppressed. This can be accomplished only by changing the economic, social, and political conditions of life which keep the oppressed in servitude to the oppressor. Thus the structures of society must be changed and, if necessary, overthrown. The economic system of capitalism must be destroyed since its primary motive is to make a profit and not to serve the needy. The downtrodden should no longer be dependent on an economic system or a class of persons (for example, the wealthy landowners), for this only perpetuates their servitude. Thus evil is not primarily a personal sin; it is systemic, inherent in the structures of society. It is only insofar as these structures are changed that the oppressed will have a chance to achieve true humanity and dignity. Theology is not universal and monolithic. It is situational, coming out of the particular historical conditions of an oppressed people. The purpose of theology is not to understand the world; it is to change the world. Theology is not systematic thinking *about* the human condition. It is direct involvement in the process of liberating the oppressed, a continuing interplay of action and theory intertwined together.

The term used to describe this constant involvement of action and reflection is *praxis*. This term has become central to Latin American theology and its conviction that the starting point of theology is involvement in and transformation of the lives of the oppressed. There is no dualism of word and deed. Praxis is the continuing interaction between practice and theory, doing and thinking. Theology as praxis is not the search for correct thinking (orthodoxy), but rather the intermingling of thought and action (orthopraxis). In Gutiérrez's familiar words, theology is "critical reflection on praxis." Theology is not just a descriptive task. Authentic theology is an active process seeking constantly for the liberation of the oppressed.

Another important term is *conscientization* which means the process by which one is educated into the fullness of the human condition. Conscientization is the ongoing struggle on the part of the oppressed to achieve their rightful dignity and status. Thus liberation theology is participatory rather than detached. It claims to be biblically based and ecumenical in its approach. It affirms that human suffering should be the primary Christian responsibility.

Rubem Alves, a Brazilian Protestant theologian, attempts to incorporate the insights of European theologian Jürgen Moltmann into the South American situation in his book *A Theology of Human Hope* (1969). But whereas Moltmann sees the reality of hope in the promise of God as already determined by the future, Alves understands hope "as the stretching out of human consciousness, as it looks beyond the unfinishedness of 'what is'."[12] Alves considers Moltmann's view too transcendental in terms of the divine promise, with too little concern for the human role in the struggle against oppression. Poverty in South America is the result of the domination of the powerful over the weak. Human liberation will be the result of human activity in the political arena. Political humanism looks to the future and encourages humanity to become the creator of history. Alves anticipates the development of liberation theology in his concern for a politically based theology, for a "God" who is the "power for humanization." For Alves, God's entire initiative is focused on the liberation of every person. Language about God is language about those events in history that foster human liberation. Alves has traveled far beyond the position he advocated in 1969. In a largely autobiographical article written ten years later he relates how in his pilgrimage he has shifted from being first a secure pious fundamentalist to a radical political activist to one who had lost any sense of hope to one who identifies himself with the experience of captivity.

> To feel oneself captive . . . is to refuse to accept the world as it is. We are impotent. To hope for liberation in captivity is to hope for the impossible: the unexpected. In the idiom of religion it is to have trust in a God who summons things that do not exist into existence and makes the barren fruitful.[13]

The first important book published on South American liberation theology is *A Theology of Liberation: History, Politics and Salvation* (1971) by Gustavo Gutiérrez, professor of Catholic theology in Lima, Peru, a book that has been called the Magna Carta of liberation theology. Robert McAfee Brown has suggested that this book may be the most important book of the decade. However, Gutiérrez would be the first to point out that he did not "invent" liberation theology. This is a theology that has arisen out of the experience of the people, especially the "communidades de base." What Gutiérrez and others did is to help articulate their experience. Gutiérrez's book is, in his own words:

> An attempt at reflection, based on the Gospel and experiences of men and women committed to the process of liberation in the oppressed and exploited land of Latin America. It is a theological reflection born of the experience of shared efforts to abolish the current unjust situation and to build a different society, freer and more human.[14]

Gutiérrez analyzes the role of theology in the history of the Christian Church and suggests that liberation theology is a new way to do theology. He traces the roots of his method to the early centuries of the Christian era. He notes in particular the theology of history which Augustine developed in *The City of God*, an analysis of the particular historical situation and the implications that this situation had for the church. Similarly the theology of liberation begins with and takes seriously the contemporary setting in South America. Until recent times the Roman Catholic Church in South America was closely identified with the established social order. The church was for all practical purposes on the side of the oppressor. The theology of liberation seeks to break these ties. "The process of liberation requires *the active participation of the oppressed*; this certainly is one of the most important themes running through the writings of the Latin American church."[15] Gutiérrez proposes three important meanings to the word liberation, including: the political liberation of the oppressed people, liberation in the course of historical developments, and liberation from sin as a necessary prelude for a new life in Christ. Gutiérrez does not reduce the gospel to politics, as his critics sometimes charge, but understands liberation as having wider dimensions and implications for both the individual and society. Gutiérrez prefers not to use the popular word *development* with respect to the approach to oppression since he associates that word with the half-hearted efforts on the part of governments and economic powers to improve the lot of the underprivileged. He prefers the stronger word *liberation* to indicate the kinds of radical changes that need to be made by the oppressed for their own welfare. The proper role of the church is to become involved in the ongoing struggle to liberate the oppressed. The church and the theologians cannot remain neutral in this struggle. They must identify with the oppressed in their revolution and enable the oppressed to become the leaders of their own struggle.

> In the last instance we will have an authentic theology of liberation only when the oppressed themselves can freely raise their voices and express themselves directly and creatively in society and in the heart of the People of God.[16]

Gutiérrez believes that this new way of doing theology is the biblical way. He and other liberation theologians place special emphasis upon the Exodus motif. Just as God liberated the Israelites from Egyptian slavery, so, too, does this God liberate the oppressed in South America from their servitude. Both acts of God are a political action—the movement away from oppression toward a free and just society. So, too, is the liberating action of Christ the gift of God. Christ does not offer us a blueprint for our everyday behavior. Gutiérrez quotes with approval the words of Guilio Girardi.

> We must love everyone, but it is not possible to love everyone in the same way: we love the oppressed by liberating them; we love the oppressors by fighting them. We love the oppressed by liberating them from their misery, and the oppressors by liberating them from their sin.[17]

For Gutiérrez, Christ as liberator is at the vanguard of the current struggle for a just and humane society.

Gutiérrez has continued as the prime interpreter of this South American approach to theology. In an article written in 1973 he contends that liberation theology has become the major force in the Christian Church in Latin America and that henceforth it is in the realm of political action that Christians must express their faith. Does this, then, make the gospel strictly a political instrument? Gutiérrez answers:

> Yes, in the case of those who use it to serve the interests of those in power; no, in the case of those who denounce the usage on the basis of its message of liberation and gratuitous divine love. Yes, in the case of those who place themselves and the gospel in the hands of the mighty of this world; no, in the case of those who identify themselves with the poor Christ and seek to establish solidarity with the dispossessed on this continent. Yes, in the case of those who keep it shackled to an ideology that serves the capitalist system; no, in the case of those who have been set free by the gospel message and then seek to liberate it from that same captivity. Yes, in the case of those who wish to neutralize Christ's liberation by restricting or reducing it to a purely spiritual plane that has nothing to do with the concrete world of human beings; no, in the case of those who believe that Christ's salvation is so total and radical that nothing escapes it.[18]

In the summer of 1975 Gutiérrez participated in the "theology of the Americas" conference in Detroit and insisted:

> *Our* question is . . . how can we say to the poor, to the exploited classes, to the marginated races, to the despised cultures, to all the minorities, to the nonpersons—how can we say that God is love and say that all of us are, and ought to be in history, sisters and brothers. How do we say this? That is our great question.[19]

One can almost say that much of the rest of South American liberation theology is but a series of footnotes to Gustavo Gutiérrez. For although other South American theologians come from countries other than Peru, and therefore reflect their particular historical situations, the basic features of their theologies remain the same. They reaffirm Gutiérrez's basic conviction which he expressed at the ecumenical dialogue of third world theologians meeting at Dar es Salaam, Tanzania in the summer of 1976. "God is a liberating God, revealed only in the concrete historical context of liberation of the poor and oppressed."[20] Here we see a direct connection—God as "a liberating God"—with black, feminist, and other forms of liberation theology. Despite these similarities, South American liberation theologians do have different emphases, styles, and interests. For example, Hugo Assmann has a pronounced Marxist stance and is disaffected from traditional theology. José Miranda has had to leave the Catholic church in order, as he says, to be faithful to Jesus Christ. Segundo Galilea stresses the "spirituality" of liberation. Gustavo Gutiérrez remains a loyal member of the church. Liberation theology is definitely not monolithic.

Attention should be given to some other South American liberation theologians and their major writings. Enrique Dussel, a Catholic Argentinian layman exiled in Mexico, has recently contributed two popular works: *History and the Theology of Liberation* (1976) and *Ethics and the Theology of Liberation* (1978). In the former work he seeks to answer the question for theology: What does it mean to be Latin Americans? Heretofore Latin American theologians have been trained in European-oriented seminaries. But a truly Latin American theology will emerge only out of the ongoing political, economic, and cultural life of the oppressed in South America. In his later book Dussel continues his earlier theme that the worst perpetrator of the prevailing corrupt world system has been colonial domination. "This is the first sin; all the others in the system spring from it."[21] The role of the church is to commit itself to the poor. The function of theology is to be historical, concrete, committed, asystematic, and prophetic. Most of Dussel's major writings—especially his massive work on the history of the church in Latin America—have not yet been translated into English.

José Miguez Bonino, a Methodist professor of theology and ethics on the faculty of the Evangelical Theologate in Buenos Aires, Argentina, has written one of the most readable accounts of South American theological developments in his book *Doing Theology in a Revolutionary Situation* (1975). This is an important survey of the historical content and the thinking of South America's leading theologians. Miguez, who served as a Protestant observer at Vatican II, contends that the Marxist view of history illuminates the public area of conflict. He champions socialism as the vehicle of Latin American liberation and declares, in support of Karl Marx, that the proper role for theology is to transform rather than to understand the world. *"Orthopraxis,* rather than orthodoxy, becomes the criterion for theology.''[22] Class struggle is a fact of life and Christians are called to participate in this struggle by identifying with the oppressed.

Juan Luis Segundo, a Jesuit priest from Uruguay, has contributed a long list of writings, including fifteen books. His latest, *The Liberation of Theology* (1976), is one of his most important. He contends that the theology of liberation:

> represents a point of no return in Latin America. It is an irreversible thrust in the Christian process of creating a new consciousness and maturity in our faith. Countless Christians have committed themselves to a fresh and radical interpretation of their faith, to a new re-experiencing of it in their real lives. And they have done this not only as isolated individuals but also as influential and sizeable groups within the Church.[23]

Segundo articulates a new process theological methodology in the spirit of the developing Latin American thinking. His views resemble those of Pierre Teilhard de Chardin. For Segundo, the interpretation of the Bible must constantly change to reflect the continuing changes in our present-day reality. Liberation, he contends, has less to do with content and more to do with the method used to theologize about one's real-life situation. Thus theology is less an academic subject and more a revolutionary activity that seeks to change the world. Segundo refers with approval to James Cone for his notion of theology as "passionate language" and for his conviction that black theology must not be abstractly universal, but accountable only to the black community. The Bible is not the proclamation of a universal God to a universal humanity, but a particular message to a particular human community, and must not hesitate to acknowledge its basis in political action. Theology and politics are inextricably intertwined. In other words,

> There is no such thing as Christian theology or a Christian interpretation of the gospel message in the absence of a prior political commitment. Only the latter makes the former possible at all.[24]

Space does not permit further comment on the views of other South American theologians. Hugo Assmann of Brazil, exiled in Costa Rica, Leonardo Boff from Brazil, Segundo Galilea of Chile, and the already mentioned Rubem Alves of Brazil are some other important names in liberation theology. Jon Sobrino, a Jesuit from El Salvador, has recently published *Christology at the Crossroads: A Latin American Approach* (1978), which argues that Jesus was very much involved in a political and social context similar to that of contemporary South America. The recently published *Frontiers of Theology in Latin America* (1979), edited by Rosino Gibellini, contains articles by most of the leading South American liberation theologians. However, this trend in theology is still so new that many books and articles by these thinkers have yet to be translated into English.

One of the turning points in black theology occurred when black theologians began to enter into critical dialogue with one another concerning the proper relationship of the Christian faith to black power, to "white" theology, and to the African heritage. A similar dialogue among South American theologians is at the beginning stages. Juan Luis Segundo, in his *The Liberation of Theology*, is critical of Hugo Assmann for seeming to assert that Christians have no distinctive contribution to make in the struggle for liberation. And he faults Rubem Alves both for his undue dependence on Jürgen Moltmann and for his rejection—as violence prone—of cooperation with revolutionary movements. Some are beginning to ask whether liberation theology has been too closely identified with Marxist categories for its explanation and solution of economic and political conflicts. José Profino Miranda's *Marx and the Bible* (1974) sought to justify the close alliance between Marx and the Bible in affirming God as the liberator of the oppressed. Segundo Galilea, now of Colombia, has warned against the charge that liberation theology "has been infiltrated by Marxism and that it leads to "horizontalism," pure politicism, and a merely temporal humanism."[25] Hugo Assmann's book *Theology for a Nomad Church* (1976) questions whether orthodox Marxism can be applied to the Latin American situation. José Miguez Bonino's *Christians and Marxists* (1976) is a careful analysis of the complexity of meaning attached to Christianity and Marxism and their interrelationships. It is to be expected that as Latin American theologians increase their critique of one another, the same crisis will develop that has occurred in black theology.

Latin American liberation theology has begun to come under attack by other theologians. A few examples will suffice. In his book *Latin American Theology: Radical or Evangelical?* (1970) C. Peter Wagner evaluates this new theology from a conservative evangelical point of view. Wagner had the benefit of living in South America in the 1960s and noted three rather distinct camps in Christianity in South America: the fundamentalist Protestants, the conservative Catholics, and the left-wing radical group composed of both Catholics and Protestants. He criticizes this third group for being too syncretistic and for seeming to adopt a socio-economic position without theological foundations. He criticizes Rubem Alves for his over-emphasis on Marxism and social revolution and for his suggestion that it might be advantageous if the church went out of existence. Wagner is equally critical of Richard Shaull for secularizing theology and for suggesting that theology needs to be crucified in the hopes that a new theological resurrection might happen. Wagner regrets that Marxist ideology has come to dominate the left wing of the Latin American church. He goes on to say:

> The important issue is not really whether a Christian can hold a Marxist-oriented political ideology or not. The issue is whether Christianity obliges a man set free in Christ to hold to *any* predetermined ideology at all. The Christian world view transcends all social, economic, and political systems. As long as a Christian's goals in his relationship to the world are noble and held with a clean conscience, he should be allowed to choose the political means to reach the goals that he feels are best without his very Christianity being called into question. . . . This applies equally to the capitalist and the socialist, the pacifist and the violent revolutionary.[26]

Wagner believes that liberation theology—or the radical left, as he terms it—has made the social revolution primary and consequently "accommodation to the 'reality presuppositions of our age' is nothing less than devastating to Christian theology."[27]

Hans Küng's major work, *On Being a Christian* (1976), levels some criticisms at liberation theology, especially for its tendency to ally itself with a particular political ideology or social program.

> For Latin-American Christians, the discussion on the political-social realization of the impulse to liberation centers on the question: does not the commitment to liberation necessarily mean a political option for *socialism* against *capitalism*? The widespread sympathy for socialism particularly

among active Christians is often the only political way out of the outrageous conditions set up in this continent as a result of the capitalist economic system.[28]

Küng notes that liberation theology has produced no concrete models for a socialist society, that at most there is a rather vague advocacy of socialism. A socialist system, like a capitalist one, is not immune to defects and misuse. Christians can be committed to liberation and yet not accept the remedy of socialization. A Christian can be a socialist, but need not be, and the liberation theologian must be careful not to identify the churches with a partisan political party. Küng is also critical of the tendency on the part of liberation theology to condone violence in order to remove an oppressive economic system—a charge which Robert McAfee Brown claims the facts do not warrant.[29] Küng uses Jesus as the model of the true revolutionary who went beyond the alternative of acquiescence to the status-quo or political revolution. He maintains that Jesus teaches

love of enemies instead of their destruction; unconditional forgiveness instead of retaliation; readiness to suffer instead of using force; blessing for peacemakers instead of hymns of hate and revenge.[30]

Jürgen Moltmann, in his "An Open Letter to José Miguez Bonino," responds directly to the latter's book *Doing Theology in a Revolutionary Situation* (1975). He insists that it is high time that European theologians meet head-on the critique of them made by Latin American theologians.

After you, Rubem Alves, Juan Segundo, Gustavo Gutiérrez, and Hugo Assmann, have made crystal clear what you find dissatisfying in us and what in our theology seems so irrelevant for your situation, I would like to begin to clarify what we find dissatisfying in you and what we actually are expecting from you.[31]

Moltmann levels two major charges against Miguez and the other South American theologians. First, they tend to be provincial in seeking to be indigenous. That is, while they rightfully seek to develop their own theology in terms of their own South American situation, they refuse to enter into constructive dialogue with their European counterparts. Moltmann reminds them that their heroes Marx and Engels are not Latin American discoveries! Further, he states that although the

South American theologians are highly critical of the political theology and theology of hope of their European counterparts, for example, Moltmann and Metz, they really end up advocating the same views. Moltmann asserts "Gutiérrez's *A Theology of Liberation* presents the process of liberation in Latin America as the continuation and culmination of the European history of freedom. . . . But where is Latin America in it all?"[32] Second, Moltmann is critical of the use of Marxism by these theologians. They quote Marx profusely and positively, but they do not analyze the class struggle with respect to the struggle of their own people. They write more about the sociological theories of others, namely Western Socialists, than about the oppression of South Americans. Third, the historical situations in South America and Europe are vastly different. In Europe, socialism and democracy go hand in hand. "Socialism without democracy, economic justice without realization of human rights are not hopes among our people."[33] The democratic way to socialism is the proper way in Europe. Whether the reverse process advocated in South America—from socialism to democracy—will work, remains to be seen. Moltmann ends with a plea for Latin American and European theologians to recognize their different historical and political situations and enter into creative discussion.

Thomas G. Sanders criticizes what he calls the "moralistic ideology" of liberation theology. He defines moralistic ideology as the analysis of each situation in terms of clear-cut evils and equally clear-cut solutions.[34] Sanders, following the views of Reinhold Niebuhr at this point, declares that this kind of thinking does not recognize the moral ambiguity inherent in every social system. South American liberation theology is naive in sharply dividing society into the good guys and the bad guys, the oppressed and the oppressor, the socialists and the capitalists. The end result is utopian rationalization, praising the partisan actions of socialist governments and condemning the policies of other governments that are not avowedly socialist. Sanders suggests that liberation theology needs to become more realistic about the ambiguities of life and the strengths and weaknesses of the various political systems and not try to make the Christian faith fit neatly into a partisan political program. Meanwhile, Sanders has been strongly criticized by Rubem Alves for distorting liberation theology as moralistic and utopian. Alves characterizes Sanders' Christian realism as an American ideology having "unambiguous relationships with colonialism, racism, and economic exploitation."[35]

Rosemary Ruether has raised the question whether liberation theologians, both black and South American, have over-stressed the role of the oppressed over against the oppressor. By raising the question of the liberation of both oppressor and oppressed she places the theology of liberation in a universal context which encompasses the "outer history" of humankind. For this reason she is worth quoting at some length.

> They must also keep somewhere in the back of their minds the idea that the dehumanization of the oppressor is really their primary problem, to which their own dehumanization is related primarily in a relationship of effect to cause. . . . Quite simply, what this means is that one cannot dehumanize the oppressors without ultimately dehumanizing oneself, and aborting the possibilities of the liberation movement into an exchange of roles of oppressor and oppressed.[36]

Ruether continues:

> All theologies of liberation, whether done in a black or a feminist or a Third World perspective, will be abortive of the liberation they seek, unless they finally go beyond the apocalyptic, sectarian model of the oppressor and the oppressed. The oppressed must rise to a perspective that affirms a universal humanity as the ground of their own self-identity, and also to a power for self-criticism. The alienated oppressor must learn what it means to be truly responsible for who and what he is.[37]

Ruether's criticism is extremely important. For, just as some black theologians have tended only to talk to one another and insist that nothing worthwhile can come from prejudiced "white" theologians, so, too, have some South American liberation theologians condemned European world theologians as academic, detached, and a tool of cultural imperialism.

Schubert M. Ogden in his book *Faith and Freedom: Toward a Theology of Liberation* (1979) sees four weaknesses in current liberation theologies: 1) they are more the rationalization of a position already taken rather than the product of critical reflection; 2) they focus almost exclusively on the existential meaning of God without dealing with the metaphysical being of God; 3) they fail to distinguish properly between the dimensions of God as redeemer and emancipator; and 4) they have too narrow a view of the forms of bondage from which humankind needs to be emancipated. Ogden opts for a process metaphysics "that goes beyond all the usual metaphysical alternatives and provides the very resources that are required if the project of a theology of liberation is to be carried out to completion."[38] However, Ogden's book seems less a careful critique of liberation theology, than a philosophical analysis of freedom and a plea for these theologians to turn to Whitehead and process theology.

The Medellin Conference of 1968 (Celam II) did indeed spark a new vision of theology in South America. A "Christians for Socialism" movement emerged in Chile in 1972 and grassroots congregations proliferated throughout the continent, advancing the social teachings advocated at Celam II. Worker-peasant groups spread and led to what is called the "popular church" movement, churches within churches advocating and practicing radical social change. However, reactionary forces also gained strength in a concerted attempt to undermine the results of the Medellin gathering. Celam III was scheduled to be held at Puebla, Mexico, in the fall of 1978. However, with the death of Pope Paul VI this conference was postponed and was not convened until early in 1979 under the leadership of the new Pope John Paul II.

Proponents and opponents of the Medellin conclusions marshalled their forces in preparation for the new conference. In 1973 the conservative Colombian bishop Alfonso Lopez Trujilla was appointed the new Secretary General and he actively sought to reverse the social teachings of Medellin. His book *Liberation or Revolution? An Examination of the Priest's Role in the Socio-Economic Class Struggle in Latin America* (1977) contends that, in advocating violent Marxist revolution, liberation theologians have reduced Christianity to radical politics. A preliminary document for Celam III was widely circulated, a document which, in the words of Robert McAfee Brown, was "a disaster to those who take Medellin seriously."[39] Gustavo Gutiérrez criticized this document as "retreat from commitment" and complained that it betrayed a European bias.

> We find that when we look at what it feels are the great problems that "touch the very heart of Christian civilization," poverty is not among them, nor are exploitation and social injustice, nor even the fact that these things are actually happening within countries "that call themselves Christian." . . .

The issues we find discussed, although certainly real issues, have a distinctly "academic" flavor.[40]

Celam III was held in Puebla, Mexico, with Pope John Paul II opening the conference. In his address he tried to steer a middle course, denouncing violence and direct participation on the part of the clergy in partisan politics while condemning social injustice and insisting that the church must be directly involved in overcoming the evils of oppression. The final document produced at Puebla was somewhat contradictory in trying to placate both conservatives and liberals. But it did advocate a degree of activism. And the liberation theologians like Gustavo Gutiérrez, Leonard Boff, Jon Sobrino, and Hugo Assmann, although not there as official delegates, were much in evidence behind the scenes, constantly in touch with the liberal bishops and other delegates. Yet Celam III did not have the dramatic impact of Celam II. In the words of Panamanian bishop Marcus McGrath:

> Medellin was a prophetic voice that didn't allow itself to be a mirror, reflecting the reality of Latin America. Puebla, on the other hand, articulates the reality of Latin America but has not allowed itself to be a prophetic message.[41]

There are definite signs that South American liberation theologians are beginning to discern the wider implications for human liberation in other parts of the world. The "Theology in the Americas" conference held in Detroit in the summer of 1975 brought together South American, black, and feminist theologians. This open confrontation of theologians operating out of different contexts of oppression was a healthy eye-opener for everyone who participated. As José Portino Miranda put it:

> We do not intend that our liberation theology is the only possible liberation theology; we do not intend to impose anything at all. I can only express my wish and my hope that out of this meeting comes a fuller and richer Christian faith and Christian action.[42]

Similarly, an ecumenical dialogue of third world theologians at Dar es Salaam in the summer of 1976 brought together twenty-two theologians from Africa, Asia, and Latin America. The final statement of this conference echoed the differences.

While the need for economic and political liberation was felt to offer a vital basis for theologizing in some areas of the Third World, theologians from other areas tended to think that the presence of other religions and cultures, racial discrimination and domination, and related situations such as the presence of Christian minorities in predominantly non-Christian societies, reveal other equally challenging dimensions of the theological task.[43]

By making these contacts with theologians from all parts of the world, the Latin American theologians are expanding their vision of liberation. They are discovering that, although the "inner history" of each indigenous political group is as important as the "inner history" of each race of people, there is also an equally important "outer history" which cuts across political boundaries, races, sexes, and nationalities. A partisan view of human liberation based solely on a socio-economic system that ignores racial and sexual oppression will end up as self-defeating as a partisan view of human liberation based on race that ignores social-economic and sexual oppression. Then, too, a view of God that tends to identify God exclusively with human—especially political—involvement ignores the metaphysical dimensions of the reality of God. Who God is, is as important as what God does.

Admittedly the results of the Puebla Conference of 1979 were not overly encouraging for liberation theology. John Eagleson and Philip Scharper have recently edited *Puebla and Beyond*, which includes both the documents produced by the conference and interpretive commentaries. The general consensus of the liberation theologians is that, in the words of Robert McAfee Brown, "It could have been a lot worse."[44] But the following passage from the conference to the peoples of Latin America testifies to what liberation theology is all about.

The civilization of love rejects subjection and dependence prejudicial to the dignity of Latin America. We do not accept the status of satellite to any country in the world, or to any country's ideology. We wish to live fraternally with all nations, because we repudiate any sort of narrow, incredible nationalism. It is time that Latin America advised the developed nations not to immobilize us, not to put obstacles in the way of our progress, and not to exploit us. Instead they would do well to help us magnanimously to overcome the barriers of our under-development while respecting our culture, our principles, our sovereignty, our identity, and our natural resources. It is in this spirit that we will grow together as fellow members of the same universal family.[45]

5

Feminist Theology

Feminist theology is largely a phenomenon of the 1970s that emerged from the larger parallel drive for women's liberation in the social-economic arena. To be sure, this drive for women's liberation was not a brand new phenomenon that appeared only in the last decade. The women's movement has had a long history, especially in the United States. The feminists in the nineteenth century sought to support the role of women in many different areas of society and, like their counterparts today, blamed the oppression of women on the oppressor man. In 1895 Elizabeth Cady Stanton edited *The Women's Bible,* her biblical commentary documenting the deep religious roots of the economic and social oppression of women. However, the major drive for women's rights came to a virtual standstill in the 1920s with the ratification of the Nineteenth Amendment which gave women the right to vote, and it was not until the 1960s that the feminist movement reasserted itself to any significant degree.

In 1961 President John F. Kennedy established the President's Commission on the Status of Women to make recommendations for overcoming the "prejudices and outmoded customs [that] act as barriers to the full realization of women's basic rights." Its report, issued two years later, though traditionalist in assigning to women the major responsibility for child rearing and homemaking, was an important impetus for the growing women's movement. In 1966 the National Organization of Women (NOW) was founded with Betty Friedan as the first president. Friedan's book *The Feminine Mystique* (1963) was perhaps the most important catalyst for women's liberation in the early 1960s. The avowed purpose of NOW was "to take action to bring women into full participation in the mainstream of American society *now*, expressing all the privileges and responsibilities thereof in truly equal partnership with men."[1] The intent of NOW was to call into question the traditional stereotypes of the role of women: that women must make a choice between marriage and work outside the home and that the husband should be the primary source of support.

What began as a trickle in the 1960s became a raging stream for the rights of women in the 1970s. This trend is particularly obvious with respect to the proper role of women in the churches and in the emergence of what is called feminist theology. For it was not until the 1970s that women in large numbers began to question male-dominated theological assumptions, including the beliefs that the subordination of woman has been ordained by God, that woman is evil by nature, and that God is male. Once again this was not the first time that these assumptions had been challenged. Some churches had already made significant progress in urging equal treatment for women and a few denominations had acknowledged the rights of women for more than a century. In 1950 the World Council of Churches, founded only two years earlier, established the Commission on the Life and Work of Women in the Church to study the role of women in the member churches. In 1956 the Methodist and Presbyterian churches gave full clergy rights to women.

One of the first major articles published in the area of feminist theology was Valerie Saiving's "The Human Situation: A Feminine View" (1960). Saiving's contention is that the theologian's sexual identity has much to do with how he or she perceives the proper role of theology, and that historically theology has been based on a male perception which has not only ignored the uniqueness of women's experience, but also strengthened the usual stereotype of women as inferior to men. Saiving declares that her purpose is

> to awaken theologians to the fact that the situation of women, however similar it may appear on the surface of our contemporary world to the situation of man . . . is, at bottom, quite different—that the specifically feminine dilemma is, in fact, precisely the opposite of the masculine. . . . If it is true that our society is moving from a masculine to a feminine orientation, then theology ought to reconsider its estimate of the human condition and redefine its categories of sin and redemption. For a feminist society will have its own special potentialities for good and evil, to which a theology based solely on masculine experience may well be irrelevant.[2]

These views were far ahead of the times, as most of the books written in the early and middle 1960s on women and religion were conservative and traditionalist in tone. A few examples will suffice. In Elizabeth Achtemeier's book *The Feminist Crisis in Christian Faith* (1965) the author writes of the contributions made by women to the social programs of the church. She complains about the extremes of the "professional" feminists and asserts "It is true that we American women still find our principal joys within the context of our homes. We would not trade our role as wives and mothers for any other or any thing." Her stereotyped conservative view of the role of women becomes even more apparent in this statement: "The Christian woman can be tastefully dressed and run a well-furnished house. If she is a good cook or a polished hostess or an accomplished conversationalist, she will delight all who know her."[3]

That same year in an article entitled "Neither Male nor Female" Doris and Howard Hunter plead for a larger role in the church for the woman theological student and say of such a person that she need not be masculine in appearance and personality.[4] "Religion and the Feminine Mystique" by Hannah Bonsey Suthers, also published in 1965, applies Betty Friedan's views to the role of women in the church and urges women to avoid the evangelical double standard and "embrace their biological function without frustration or rationalization."[5] Elsie Thomas Culver's *Women in the World of Religion* (1967) summarizes the historical record of women in the field of religion, noting that the idea of a woman having anything important to say theologically was as inconceivable to the sixteenth-century reformers as it would be to contemporary churches.[6] However, the establishment of the women's caucus at the General Assembly of the National Council of Churches in Detroit in 1969 indicates the spread of more progressive views of the role of women. This caucus declared:

> Women's oppression and women's liberation is a basic part of the struggle of blacks, browns, youth, and others. We will not be able to create a new church and a new society until and unless women are full participants. We intend to be full participants . . . "the next great movement in history" will be ours.[7]

The first major widely publicized book on the role of women and the church that hints at the formulation of a specifically feminist theology is *The Church and the Second Sex* (1968) by Mary Daly. Although Daly has since become much more radical in her own views, in her first book she is able to articulate a feminist stance that receives a wide hearing. Daly examines the oppression of women by the Church as understood by Simone de Beauvior in her classic study *The Second Sex*. She maintains that the Church has encouraged the view of women as inferior (a "defective male," as St. Thomas Aquinas put it) and that it has been a leading instrument of the oppression of women. Daly asserts that it was the industrial revolution and not the Church that led to female emancipation.[8] But she does admit that Vatican II has given women increased hopes for equality. Indeed Daly claims that the fundamental difference between her and de Beauvior is the latter's despair and her own hope that the Church can bring about a radical transformation of the lives of women.

Since the publication of *The Church and the Second Sex*, the market has been flooded with writings on feminist theology. There is no adequate way of summarizing the scope of these contributions. Feminist theology has had no organizing theme, no obvious focus, no sharply identifiable set of objectives. To be sure, it is one in its opposition to the maleness of God and tradition, and the consequent subordination of women. But it has lacked a model for tackling these issues in a clear and systematic manner. It has often been divided on the question of whether, for example, these issues should be settled by the reinterpretation or complete rejection of male language, by the renewal or overthrow of religious tradition, by cooperation with or the snubbing of the male sex, and so on. All that we can do here is to single out a few of the leading feminist theologians and some of their major writings to indicate the directions in which this discipline seems to be moving.

Mary Daly's views have been steadily radicalized as suggested above. By 1971 she had begun to move outside the boundaries of the Roman Catholic Church to search for concepts and language more closely identifiable with the growing feminist movement. That year she designated the idea of "sisterhood" as crucial, urging the need for "the bonding of those who have never been bonded before for the purpose of overcoming sexism and its effects, both internal and external.'"[9] In 1973 Daly published her second book, *Beyond God the Father: Toward a Philosophy of Women's Liberation,* which she sees as a sequel to her earlier book. Here she continues her quest for radically different terminology and develops the concept of *naming* as important for women, insisting that the liberation of women must include a "castrating of language and images that reflect and perpetuate the structures of a sexist world."[10] This recasting of language does not mean merely an exchange of words—from "he" to "she" concerning God, for example—but a deeper transformation in the meaning of God, from that of noun to verb, as the Be-ing in which we participate. She considers the verb to be more personal, dynamic, and active. She asserts that women need to engage in a radical kind of consciousness-raising that will give them a new vision of their own authentic natures. In her continuing movement away from the Catholic church Daly further develops the concept of sisterhood as "the Antichurch," as the female effort to rename the cosmos. She considers herself engaged in a postchristian spiritual revolution in which old terms are given radically new meanings. Her intention to reconstruct the traditional male language and radically reinterpret Christian terminology is seen in this example.

> Seen from a certain perspective the Antichrist and *The Second Coming of Women* are synonymous. The Second Coming is not a return of Christ but a new arrival of female presence, once strong and powerful but enchained since the dawn of patriarchy. Only *this* arrival can liberate the memory of Jesus from the enchainment to the role of mankind's most illustrious scapegoat.[11]

In 1975 Daly published a revised edition of *The Church and the Second Sex* which includes a "new feminist postchristian" introduction which is intended to show how the new Daly differs radically from the old. She describes her earlier work as "band-aid" treatment, as a refusal to say "No" to the institution of the church and a resounding "Yes" to the incarnate movement of sisterhood, as a futile accommodating attempt to gain "partnership" with men since it is impossible to dialogue with the oppressor. So since 1975 Daly has made a complete break with the Catholic church, despite the fact that she continues to teach at a Catholic institution, Boston College. She has disavowed any hope of working in equal partnership with men in the church. She has changed from a reforming Catholic to a postchristian feminist who now wonders why anyone would want equality in the church, for that "would be comparable to a black person's demanding equality in the Ku Klux Klan."[12] Her avowed intention is to seek a new vision that is rooted exclusively in women's experience. She wants to discover what is distinctive about female experience and what this says about women's relationship to the cosmos. To quote her:

> . . . what women require is *ludic cerebration,* the free play of intuition in our own space, giving rise to thinking that is vigorous, informed, multidimensional, independent, creative, tough. Ludic cerebration is thinking out of experience. I do not mean the experience of dredging out All That Was Wrong with Mother or of instant intimacy in group encounters or of waiting at the doctoral dispensary or of self-lobotomization in order to publish, perish, and then be promoted. I mean the experience of be-ing. Be-ing is the verb that says the dimensions of depth in all verbs, such as intuiting, loving, imaging, making, acting, as well as the couraging, hoping, and playing that are always there when one is really living.[13]

Daly's latest book is *Gyn/Ecology: The Metaethics of Radical Feminism* (1978). Here she even goes beyond *Beyond God the Father* in two respects. First, she continues to develop new language that spins beyond Christianity and, second, she explicitly rejects certain language as "male-functioning."

> Three such words in *Beyond God the Father* which I cannot use again are *God, androgyny,* and *homosexuality.* There is no way to remove male/ masculine imagery from *God.* Thus, when writing/speaking "anthropomorphically" of ultimate reality, of the divine spark of be-ing, I now choose to write-speak gynomorphically. I do so because *God* represents the necrophilia of patriarchy, whereas *Goddess* affirms the life-loving be-ing of women and nature. The second semantic abomination, *androgyny,* is a confusing term which I sometimes used in attempting to describe integrity of be-ing. The word is misbegotten—conveying something like "John Travolta and Farrah Fawcett-Majors scotch-taping together" . . . The third treacherous term, *homosexuality,* reductionally "includes," that is, excludes gynocentric being/Lesbianism.[14]

Daly now contends that men are inferior to women and that women should become "Revolting Hags" who seek to affirm their original birth out of the inner mystery of the Other. "This book is an act of Dis-possession, and hence . . . it is absolutely Anti-androcrat, A-mazingly Anti-male, Furiously and Finally Female."[15] Daly denounces Christian feminists as "roboticized tokens" who play into the hands of phallocentric male supremacists and suggests that only lesbian radical feminists can rise above the normal way of life of the patriarchal male and "spin deeper into the listening deep."[16] If Daly's language and concepts have become strange and often incomprehensible it is because she has deliberately made them so. It is her pedagogical device to indicate that she has divorced herself from tradition. Her break with the church, with male theologians, with classical theology, and with Christian feminists is now complete.

Mary Daly represents only a small segment of feminist theologians who urge a blatant reverse sexism that is not only man-hating but also against all women who do not follow them. A more moderate approach is taken by Rosemary Radford Ruether who remains a committed Roman Catholic and yet an equally committed feminist. Her theological interests have been much more eclectic than Daly who writes almost exclusively on strictly feminist concerns. Ruether also keeps in closer dialogue with mainstream theologians (including men) than Daly, who seems uninterested in communicating with persons, male and female, who have viewpoints other than her own. Ruether takes a much more political-economic analytic starting point than does Daly and favors a methodology that stresses the interlocking of economic, social, racial, and sexual factors. However, it is true that in the past five years Ruether has devoted herself more to specifically women's issues than she did earlier.

In 1970 Ruether was already comparing the rise of the women's movement with black liberation. She noted that women and blacks originally tried to harmonize their interests with their oppressor but soon realized that to achieve authentic liberation they first had to find their own distinctive identity. For Ruether, there is a common destiny for all oppressed groups, namely, to rediscover their own inner history and reintegrate into their lives those special qualities which had been lost. Whereas Ruether sees a close affinity between women's and black liberation, Daly is critical of black theology. For example, Daly declares:

> In the "black theology" of James Cone, for example, we find a Black God and a Black Messiah, but this pigmentation operation does not significantly alter the behavior of Jahweh and Son. Cone's Black God is as revengeful and sexist as his White prototype. For feminist eyes it is clear that this God is at least as oppressive as the old.[17]

To this charge Ruether replies:

> It seems to me impossible for the black movement to respond to the sort of feminist theology represented by Mary Daly's recent book *Beyond God the Father,* for example. The liberation symbols of this book are mostly mariological. Virginity, immaculate conception, and the assumption are held up as the symbols of feminine superiority. The judgmental symbol . . . is that of castration. For black society, both of these symbols are totally encapsulated in white racism . . . such symbols seem simply expressions of white sexual pathology.[18]

Unlike Daly, who sees no point in working with or for men, Ruether is also concerned that all oppressed groups—for example, women and blacks—bear a responsibility to liberate the oppressor. In 1972 she wrote:

> To the extent that they (oppressed groups) are not at all concerned about maintaining an authentic prophetic address to the oppressors; to the extent that they repudiate them as persons . . . and conceive of liberation as a mere reversal of this relationship . . . they both abort their possibilities as a liberating force for the oppressors, and, ultimately, derail their own power to liberate themselves.[19]

Ruether's more recent writings have dealt more specifically with the issue of sexism: *Religion and Sexism: Images of Woman in the Jewish and Christian Traditions* (1974), *From Machismo to Mutuality: Essays on Sexism and Woman/Man Liberation* (1975), *New Women, New Earth: Sexist Ideologies and Human Liberation* (1975), and *Mary: The Feminine Face of The Church* (1978). Yet it is significant to note that the issue of sexism for Ruether is always seen in the context of other forms of oppression. For example, her essays on *New Women, New Earth* represent Ruether's attempt to look at the interrelationship of sexism with other forms of oppression such as racism, class structure, and technological power. She insists that if the feminist movement concerns itself only with sexism, it will remain a movement of the white upper class.[20] Her book *From Machismo to Mutuality* was coauthored with Eugene Bianchi (Can one imagine Mary Daly ever coauthoring a book with a male?) and contends that sexism must be related to the deeper forms of oppression which are also expressed in racism, militarism, and totalitarianism. Her concern, then, is to develop a feminist theology which will seek a community of mutuality between women and men, "not a rejectionist community of women that impugns the humanity of men." Ruether calls this latter position more immature than radical, adding:

That humiliated people succumb to desires for revenge is understandable; it is "only human." But it is not what I want to call "feminist ethics."[21]

Ruether's latest book, *Women of Spirit: Female Leadership in the Jewish and Christian Traditions* (1979), is a collection of articles by various feminist theologians who seek to recover significant aspects of women's history heretofore ignored by male writers. However, Ruether's concern is not only to uncover suppressed historical data on the role of women, but to seek insights for a new vision of women in leadership roles for the present and future. Women should not merely imitate male models but reshape these models into ones that are more open and dynamic. Ruether sees sexism as emanating from false dualisms in Western ways of thinking: being-becoming, mind-body, life-death, spirituality-carnality, and the like. These dualsims, so much an integral part of Hellenic ways of thinking since the time of the early church and incorporated into the church creeds and catechisms, have been socially stereotyped on male and female. The female has been identified with the lower self as body, carnality, and death, and therefore, judged inferior to the male. Only when this false dualism can be overcome will sexism be eradicated.

In an article in *Christianity and Crisis* Carter Heyward notes that Mary Daly and Rosemary Ruether are the most famous proponents in this country of two sharply different feminist theological points of view. Heyward compares underlying assumptions of these two feminists. She suggests that Daly, as we have also noted, has deliberately chosen to remove herself from the normal world of discourse and go it on her own in shaping views commensurate with her own personal experience. "Daly provokes my fist to clench, my stomach to spasm, my silent voice to shriek No!" On the other hand, Ruether remains a Roman Catholic in the mainstream of philosophical and theological discourse and places women's liberation in the larger framework of human oppression, a strategy that Heyward approves. "Ruether evokes my nod, my commitment, my Yes!"[22]

Although Daly and Ruether may be the most important representatives of two foci of feminist theology today, other women are making major contributions in this area in their own distinctive way. Letty Russell has several books to her credit including *Human Liberation in a Feminist Perspective, a Theology* (1974), *The Liberating Word: A Guide to Nonsexist Interpretation of the Bible* (1976), and *The Future of Partnership* (1979).

In the first-mentioned book Russell follows Ruether in suggesting that the exploitation of women is but one significant aspect of many forms of oppression: racism, capitalism, etc. "Feminist theology strives to be *human* and not just *feminine,* as other forms of theology should strive to be *human* and not just masculine."[23] Feminist theology, like other types of liberation theology, arises out of a particular experience of oppression and seeks through an approach that is inductive and experimental in nature to produce changes that will lead to economic, political, and social equality of the sexes. Russell believes that a misunderstanding of the nature of biblical religion has led to a conflict with feminism, and therefore she takes pains to ground her feminism in a proper view of scripture. Russell shows an affinity with South American liberation theology by utilizing its terminology—for example, praxis, conscientization, orthopraxy—to express the three ingredients of human wholeness for which all forms of liberation theology are striving: the search for true humanity, the way to servanthood, and the importance of partnership. It is this latter point that Russell develops in her latest book, *The Future of Partnership*.

> In our journey of faithfulness with God and others, we find not one partner but many partners. None of us is single. . . . Partnership for Christians is described in this book as *a new focus of relationship in a common history of Jesus Christ that sets persons free for others.*[24]

Russell writes as a deeply committed Christian who uses biblical insights to struggle for new life styles of equality between men and women and to learn to care creatively for one another in a society "that is prefigured in the coming of Christ and opened up by the promise and actions of God."[25] Phyllis Trible's *God and the Rhetoric of Sexuality* (1978) examines the issue of sexist presuppositions in the scripture in a manner similar to Letty Russell. She uses the metaphor "male and female" as the proper meaning of the "image of God" to develop a biblical hermeneutics of feminism.

If Letty Russell is hopeful in advocating a partnership with men,

Sheila Collins is more critical of male theologians for their failure to distinguish between the essence of religious faith and cultural accretions. In an article entitled "Toward a Feminist Theology" she faults the church for conveying the scriptures as an image of the male experience of the surrounding world. "In both Old and New Testament times women were regarded as an inferior species to be owned like cattle, as unclean creatures incapable of participating in the mysteries of the worship of Yahweh."[26] Like Ruether and Russell, Collins sees a parallel between feminist and black theology—both emerge from oppressed groups. And she looks forward to the day when "men discover their femininity and women their masculinity" in a truly liberating partnership. These views Collins further develops in her book *A Different Heaven and Earth* (1974) in which she locates feminist theology in the center of the experience of an oppressed people, within a communal process in which women together address mutual concerns. The core of feminist theology is what she calls "a shared search for transcendence."[27] Collins opts for a new vision of history or, as she terms it, "herstory." For too long history has been understood as a record of certain facts that are "objective rather than subjective, rational rather than intuitive, linear rather than circular or organic, logical rather than mystical, dissecting rather than unifying, abstract rather than concrete."[28] "Herstory" broadens one's view of life and makes one reinterpret the ways in which the past has been understood.

> Women's herstory seeks to open up to purview the vast panorama of human experience, so that reality systems may be seen in their relationship to one another. Just as colors assume different hues depending on the colors they are surrounded by, so Judeo-Christian history and its authority systems take on a different gestalt when juxtaposed with the world view they sought to extinguish.[29]

To this end theologian Penelope Washbourn, writing in 1974, suggests that women need a new myth-model to assist them in shaping their own true identities, a myth which Washbourn finds in the symbol of the Virgin-Goddess.

> This may appear a rather surprising suggestion at a time when Women's Liberation is concerned primarily with political and economic issues and social changes. It is my contention that an ethic arises out of a myth-model and that the insufficiency of our ethic stems from the confusion of our

myth-models. The ethics of Women's Liberation need to grow from prime symbols of the feminine reality, and I hope to show how the symbol of the Virgin-Goddess embodies the essence of the female principle.[30]

For Washbourn, such a myth-model means the need for women to define their own distinctive experience, to refuse to affirm anything other than their own spirit, and to accept their own sexuality as an authentic part of the creative process. Women's selfhood has more integrity than their roles as mothers, wives, and lovers.

> In this regard I have begun to appreciate the Virgin Mary's obedience to the Spirit of God. She was not obedient to any man. The child that was born was the fruit of her dedication to the spirit within her. The Spirit of God is the feminine principle within her. She remains true to her own intentionality.[31]

However, this notion of the "myth of Mary" is strongly criticized by Elizabeth Fiorenza who claims it "has its roots and development in the male, clerical, and ascetic culture and theology."[32] Rosemary Ruether elaborates on this point:

> Mariology cannot be a liberating symbol for women as long as it preserves this meaning of "femininity" that is the complementary underside of masculine domination. Mariology becomes a liberating symbol for women only when it is seen as a radical symbol of a new humanity freed from hierarchical power relations, including that of God and humanity.[33]

In 1977 Washbourn published *Becoming Woman: The Quest for Wholeness in Female Experience* in which she analyzes the life stages of a woman's experience.

> I propose that a woman's search for psychological and spiritual wholeness goes through the life-crises of being a female body. These stages are not just psychological phases to be negotiated but turning points that raise fundamentally religious questions. At each juncture a woman must redefine her self-identity in relation to her perception of the purpose of life and in relation to her understanding of her own identity in relation to that ultimate value.[34]

Washbourn traces these female life-crises from birth to old age, indicating that there is no permanent female identity, but rather, that becoming woman is a continuously changing process in which a woman is to risk sloughing off the old and putting on the new in a never-ending quest for selfhood.

Becoming woman is a spiritual search. It involves finding a sense of one's personal worth in relation to the whole of life, even beyond death. Believing in ourselves, loving ourselves as women, is our most sacred task in and through the many phases of our sexual and personal development. Finding freedom from fear involves risking and trusting our feelings. As we risk, however, we will be given new hope, new strength, and new love for ourselves and for others. Acting on this trust will enable us to grow in understanding through all the stages of life.[35]

Penelope Washbourn writes as a Christian feminist who has an appreciation for Christian symbols yet who also seeks in the unique experience of women a new awareness of the spiritual dimension.

In recent years a plethora of books have been published that are relevant to feminist theology. Space permits mention of only a few of the significant ones. Merlin Stone in *The Paradise Papers: The Suppression of Women's Rites* (1976) tells how in the earliest known periods of human history most gods were considered female and that it was the later male-worshipping religions—for example, Judaism, Christianity, and Islam—that suppressed the female components. Stone believes that it is important to unearth these early female religions to give a more accurate description of the role and capabilities of women in ancient times. In *Behind the Sex of God: Toward a New Consciousness Transcending Matriarchy and Patriarchy* (1977) Carol Ochs reiterates Merlin Stone's assertion that patriarchal religion superseded the earlier matriarchal framework, yet Ochs points out that the matriarchal perspective continued to survive in the Grecian Eleusinian mysteries. She further contends that the union of the feminine and masculine components can enrich our notion of the nature of reality.

My position is that God is not apart from, separate from, or other than this reality. We, all together, are part of the whole, the All in All. God is not father, nor mother, nor even parents, because God is not other than, distinct from, or opposed to creation. . . . What I am suggesting is a major revolution. The revolution in knowledge and change, mind and body, matter and energy, will be joined by challenging the opposition of matriarchy and patriarchy. With this challenge will come the collapse of the opposition inherent in dualism.[36]

Rita M. Gross's collection of essays in *Beyond Androcentrism: New Essays on Women and Religion* (1977) reflects what she calls the "paradigm shift" in the academic study of religion, a shift from viewing maleness as the only bonafide expression of the human norm to a model of humanity that includes male and female, both dimensions equal though different in perceptions. "Feminist theology has shown us, through its criticism of male God-language, that while *God* may transcend and unify human experience, the theologian does not."[37] Meanwhile, in *A Socio-Theology of Letting Go: The Role of a First World Church Facing the Third World People* (1977) Marie Augusta Neal writes as a Roman Catholic from the perspective of a liberation theology that calls for another kind of shift, a "theology of relinquishment," in which the advantaged privileged peoples of the first world let go their privileges and resources in order to help the poor and oppressed organize to demand their rightful share of the world's resources and wealth. Neal moves beyond a concern with exclusively feminist issues to a vision of sexism as just one form of human oppression.

Naomi Goldenberg's *Changing of the Gods: Feminism and the End of Traditional Religions* (1979) envisages a radical recasting of the meaning and function of religious faith that will include the destruction of traditional religions. "It is likely that as we watch Christ and Yahweh tumble to the ground, we will completely outgrow the need for an external god." Goldenberg is also gently critical of some of her sister feminists, especially the reformers whom she sees "engaged in a hopeless effort." Using Jungian insights she rejects the Judeo-Christian tradition and advocates feminine witchcraft as the religion of the future. She finds in the ancient practice of witchcraft powerful symbols that can be effectively utilized for contemporary affirmations of feminism. Especially appropriate is the Mother Goddess, the source of life, who is the divine-female principle that pervades all her creation.

> My own respect for feminine witchcraft has grown over a two-year period of association with contemporary witches. I have come to understand that modern witches are using religion and ritual as psychological tools to build individual strengths. They practice a religion that places divinity or supernatural power within the person. In a very practical sense they turned religion into psychology. Witchcraft is the first modern theistic religion to conceive of its deity mainly as an internal set of images and attitudes.[38]

"Starhawk" in her *The Spiral Dance* (1979) agrees with Goldenberg and sees in witchcraft a way of eliminating false perceptions of oneself, putting one in harmony with the immanent Mother Goddess. Starhawk also stresses the ecological dimension, noting the interrelatedness among humans, animals, and plants.

Still other feminist theologians are developing different approaches. In *Women and Nature: The Roaring Inside Her* (1978) Susan Griffin notes how man has always considered himself superior to nature and to woman. Like Rosemary Ruether she protests against all those separations which form man's thinking—mind and emotion, body and soul, etc.—and like Starhawk she suggests a vision of oneness among all things. Carol Christ in her book *Diving Deep and Surfacing: Women Writers on Spiritual Quest* (1980) discusses the poetry and fiction of some women writers to illustrate her thesis that women's spiritual quest is first an experience of nothingness, then an awakening through mystical identification, and finally the discovery of a new orientation of the self integrated with nature and the cosmos. Virginia Hearn's edited work *Our Struggle to Serve* (1979) relates the stories of fifteen evangelical Christian women and how they have sought to escape from the trappings of a male-dominated church and society. Hearn's book is an important sequel to the ground-breaking work *All We're Meant to Be* (1975) by Letha Scanzoni and Nancy Hardesty, a biblical analysis of women's issues from an evangelical perspective. Finally, in *Feminine Spirituality in America* (1980) Amanda Porterfield takes as her starting point the philosopher William James's contention that the universe is friendly to the human spirit. Her thesis is that feminine spirituality—that is, one's deepest feelings of intimacy and beauty—is an important strain in the American experience—a strain which she traces in a narrative style from Puritan times to the contemporary dancer Martha Graham—a strain which includes women and men both in their home life and in their professions. What is particularly significant about this approach is its positive and expansive view of spiritual consciousness evidenced in what William James called a variety of religious experiences.

This all-too-brief survey indicates that feminist theology has branched out into many different areas: biblical, historical, social, political, and economic, as well as theological. Sometimes feminist theology has focused sharply on the issue of sexism, while at other times it has evidenced concern for other forms of human oppression in a broader understanding of liberation theology. It has taken varying and often sharply conflicting attitudes toward language, religious tradition, the role of men, and the distinctively female experience. Yet feminist theologians have tried very hard to present a united front on the grounds that "the enemy"—sexism—is so pervasive and overwhelming in all areas of society that differences must be minimized lest "the enemy" divide and conquer. Thus, to be critical of one another would be tantamount to treason. But one of the marks of a maturing point of view or society is the willingness to tolerate criticism from within, to face one another with honest differences of opinion in the hope that progress can be made through a mutual give-and-take within the same grouping. The emergence of a more adequate model and methodology for articulating a feminist theology hinges upon the potential for dialogue among feminist theologians. Fortunately there are indications that such a dialogue is beginning.

In *Women and Men: The Consequences of Power* (1977), an edited work, Dana Hiller and Robin Sheets divide feminists into four general categories: 1) *conservatives* who favor equality but still maintain the basic attitudes of society toward the family and sexuality; 2) *reformers* who are committed to major changes in these areas as well as in economic and political life and who continue to work with the present political process; 3) *politicos* whose first allegiance is to socialism and who consider feminism as but one aspect of that loyalty; and 4) *radicals* who call for fundamental revolution in restructuring society.[39] Although this classification is helpful in indicating basic differences, it fails to confront the more specific issues mentioned earlier. For example, do the politicos and radicals eliminate traditional language or invent a new one? Do they go "to the roots" and rediscover the earlier authentic tradition or discard tradition altogether?

Another important sign that feminist theologians are on the threshold of an in-house critique is the significant book *Womanspirit Rising: A Feminist Reader in Religion* (1979) edited by Carol Christ and Judith Plaskow. Although the several contributors in this collection of essays agree "that religions of the West have betrayed women," they differ significantly in their solutions to the problem. Feminists disagree with respect to "views of the past, the human relationship to nature, the character of religious community, and central religious symbols."[40] They cite disagreement as to whether traditions are irreformably sexist and patriarchal or susceptible to change; whether feminists consider themselves Jewish, post-Jewish, Christian, post-Christian, pagan, or witch; whether they can legitimately be considered historians or herstorians; whether scripture is useless or subject to reinterpretation and so on. Nevertheless, despite these differences, Christ and Plaskow contend that

> The fundamental commitment that feminists in religion share to end male ascendency in society and religion is more important than their differences. Time will tell which strategies will prove most effective in achieving the shared goal. What is clear is that, if feminists succeed, religion will never be the same again.[41]

Rosemary Ruether has recently been critical of some radical feminists. She accuses those who advocate a modern version of witchcraft of distorting historical data and trying to "top" the Jewish Holocaust in citing past atrocities against practitioners of witchcraft. She objects to Mary Daly, whose recent work seems to identify goodness with women and badness with men. Such distortion, she says, only leads to paranoia and elitism and to a false dualism which Ruether has so consistently opposed. She pleads for a feminist spirituality which can be created

> not by means of separation and rejection, but by means of synthesis and transformation. We need to work through, with great breadth and depth, what our actual experience has been, both in the dominant culture shared by males and in the suppressed experiences of women. Then we can begin to put together a new synthesis that utilizes many of the elements of earlier traditions, but within a new and liberated context.[42]

It is understandable that feminist theologians are wary about criticizing one another. All oppressed groups are eager to present a united front against the common oppressor. Moreover, a communal approach has been essential in order to establish feminist theology as a legitimate enterprise. Feminist theologians have been accused of distorting theology into a militant arm of the women's movement, of misusing theology for primarily political ends, of making theology into an ideology, in short, of over-playing feminism and diluting theology. This charge of the misuse of theology has been made against blacks and South American liberation theologians as well as women. A defensive posture for feminist theologians seems essential, at least at the early stages of a movement. However, as one goes deeper into a subject, one realizes that there is no one female or black or male or white point of view. Women disagree among themselves as much as any other group of human beings does. It is imperative, then, that feminist theologians honestly admit and confront significant differences of opinion among themselves—engage in forthright dialogue with one another in the public forum and let the chips fall where they may. Is there a distinctly feminine experience? What is it? If there is, does this create another dualism between male and female? What is the proper relationship between female and male? What is the role of the Bible and Western religious traditions? What about the Eastern traditions? Is sexism society's basic evil or is it just one important aspect of a deeper evil that encompasses economic, social, racial, and political dimensions? How do feminist concerns relate to the plight of blacks, reds, yellows, South Americans, Africans? Is there a wider all-encompassing liberation theology? These are some of the critical issues about which feminist theologians must confront one another.

6

Evangelical Theology

One of the significant features on the religious scene in the 1970s has been the conservative trend. Many individuals, unsettled by the chaos of the 1960s, have opted for a faith that will give them a sense of meaning and belonging in a world of insecurity. The result has been a dramatic rise in the number of evangelical Christians. The conservative theological movement in Christianity, as indicated earlier, emerged as a self-conscious group earlier in this century although its leaders claim that it was in substance the same basic Christian faith accepted by most Protestant believers in the nineteenth century. It reached a peak in the early 1920s with its concerted attack on Protestant liberalism which, conservatives believed, was a betrayal of the Christian gospel. Although it continued to be a potent force into the fifties and sixties, conservatism lost some of its offensive vigor as it grudgingly faced the recurring demands of a secular world. Many of its leading advocates adopted the term "evangelical" and joined together into the National Association of Evangelicals in 1942 with C. S. Lewis, Edward Carnell, and Carl Henry as their leading theoreticians. This group opposed the extremes of the fundamentalist movement yet also wanted to provide a viable alternative to the more liberal attitudes in the growing Protestant ecumenical movement.

An important indication of the turn to the right among some theologians in the 1970s was the Hartford Appeal for Theological Affirmation in 1975. This statement, signed by eighteen theologians belonging to the Roman Catholic and mainline Protestant churches, presents thirteen succinct themes characterizing the recent tendency to accommodate the Christian faith to the secular world view. In repudiating these themes, this appeal above all laments the loss of the sense of the transcendent in recent religious thought and calls for a prophetic Christian affirmation that would judge rather than accept uncritically the thought categories of the day. The Hartford Appeal struck a responsive

95

chord and, although most of the signatories were not strictly speaking conservative theologians, their support of this document betrays the conservative tone of the 1970s.

One important phase of the conservative upsurge has been fundamentalism. This movement insists upon a completely literal interpretation of the Bible and opposes efforts at cooperation or dialogue with those who depart from their version of Christian truth, even regarding minute details. Although fundamentalism has been a vigorous force in the 1970s, it will not be discussed in depth here because, due to its intransigence, it has changed very little if at all in matters of belief during the past decades. Anyone who wishes to investigate this movement would do well to read James Barr's *Fundamentalism* (1977).[1] Our interest here is in new trends in evangelicalism.

The magazine *Christianity Today* claims that twenty percent of the people in the United States are evangelicals.[2] George Gallup says thirty percent.[3] What does the term *evangelical* imply? A variety of answers can be given, depending on who is asked. Even evangelicals disagree among themselves. American church historian Sidney Ahlstrom answers in this fashion.

In contemporary American parlance the noun *evangelical* . . . refers to those Protestants who:

(1) repudiate Roman Catholic polity, liturgies, piety, and doctrine, and at least used to regard the Roman Catholic Church as the Anti-Christ;

(2) insist upon verbal inerrancy of the received biblical text, tend to interpret revelation in strict propositional terms, and question the value of historico-critical studies of biblical religion;

(3) regard the doctrine of *sola scriptura* as having very serious import for the devotional life of every Christian;

(4) emphasize the experiential dimensions of being or becoming a Christian and hence tend to diminish the significance of the sacraments, a sacerdotal clergy, authoritative hierarchical structures, and doctrinal complexities;

(5) understand the ethical teachings of the Bible in a precisionistic or legalistic manner and oppose utilitarian or situational approaches;

(6) resist the extension of fellowship or even the name of Christian to persons and churches that do not share these convictions.

This is, I believe, an uncontrived and untendentious definition of a movement which includes Christians who belong to several quite diverse confessional families. It says nothing of social or political attitudes or of philosophical positions that many evangelicals might regard as extrinsic to their theological position.[4]

It is important to distinguish fundamentalism from evangelicalism. Both movements proclaim their allegiance to biblical authority, but whereas fundamentalism resists modern critical attempts to study the Bible, evangelicalism at least attempts to take seriously the claims and results of recent scholarly study of the Bible. By the middle 1950s, evangelicalism claimed to influence the religious views of millions of American Protestants. Yet by that time it was having increasing difficulty disassociating itself from fundamentalism while, at the same time, opposing the influence of Protestant liberalism in the major Protestant denominations. Carl Henry's little book *Evangelical Responsibility in Contemporary Theology* (1957) locates some of the weaknesses of evangelical theology that had become apparent by the late 1950s, suggesting how some of these might be overcome. Henry calls Protestant liberalism a perversion of the Christian faith, yet he also criticizes fundamentalism for its opposition to the social gospel, its failure to maintain a balance among the major teachings of the Christian faith, and its extreme emphasis on premillenarianism. Henry argues that the real bankruptcy of fundamentalism is less a "reactionary spirit" than "a spirit of lovelessness" caused in large part by its over-zealous leadership. Henry goes on to say:

> One of the ironies of contemporary church history is that the more fundamentalists stressed separation from apostasy as a theme in their churches, the more a spirit of lovelessness seemed to prevail. The theological conflict with liberalism deteriorated into an attack upon organizations and personalities.[5]

Here Henry vigorously upholds the doctrinal position of evangelical theology and declares that no theology can be considered Christian if it does not affirm the deity of Christ, the virgin birth, the bodily resurrection, and the second coming of Christ. But he also insists that "evangelical responsibility in contemporary theology" must be to correct its previous defects, to enter the arena of rational debate with a less defensive approach to philosophy and the sciences, and to demonstrate a much more affirmative appreciation of the social dimensions of the Christian faith.

On this latter point Richard Pierard's study *The Unequal Yoke: Evangelical Christianity and Political Conservatism* (1970) documents how closely traditional evangelical Christianity has been identified with social and economic right-wing groups, and predicts, as Henry had done thirteen years earlier, "a crisis of disastrous proportions"[6] would follow if that alliance were to continue. Meanwhile, Carl Henry has continued to be a prime interpreter of evangelical theology. In 1956 he founded and became the first editor of the magazine *Christianity Today*, the unofficial voice of this theological camp. His edited book *Basic Christian Doctrines* (1962), a volume of essays by evangelical theologians which had appeared in *Christianity Today*, underlines the united effort by Henry and colleagues to oppose "the modern bias against the reality of the supernatural, a bias encouraged by the tenets of secularism, scientism, and naturalistic philosophy."[7] In 1977 *Time Magazine* named Henry Evangelicalism's "leading theologian."

In the 1960s evangelical theology remained a viable alternative, but it was vastly overshadowed in the public news media by the other more catchy theological fads: the death of God, secularism, the theology of hope, and so on. By the end of that decade, however, as the mood of the country shifted from action to introspection, from chaos to a search for security, from the splintering of values to the need for a sense of community, the conditions appeared ripe for a resurgence of a more conservative and solid religious faith. Richard Coleman's book *Issues of Theological Warfare: Evangelicals and Liberals* (1972) points to the growing strength of the evangelical movement and the erosion of theological liberalism. He notes the deepening division between liberal and evangelical Protestants and the increasing dissatisfaction with liberal leadership in both the ecumenical movement and the major denominations, resulting in an amazing revival of the evangelical movement in the 1970s.[8] Dean M. Kelley's influential sociological study, *Why Conservative Churches Are Growing* (1972), offers a comprehensive explanation for this evangelical upsurge, giving four features of the phenomenon.

1. Those who are serious about their faith do not confuse it with other beliefs, loyalties, or practices, or mingle them together indiscriminately, or pretend they are alike, of equal merit, or mutually compatible if they are not.

2. Those who are serious about their faith make high demands of those admitted to the organization that bears the faith, and they do not include or allow to continue within it those who are not fully committed to it.

3. Those who are serious about their faith do not consent to, encourage, or indulge any violations of its standards of belief or behavior by its professed adherents.

4. Those who are serious about their faith do not keep silent about it, apologize for it, or let it be treated as though it made no difference, or should make no difference, in their behavior or their relationships with others.

Thus, concludes Kelley:

> The very qualities that make a religious movement objectionable to critical outsiders are what make it convincing to adherents and potential converts.[9]

The pollster George Gallup, Jr., designated the year 1976 "the year of the evangelical" and believes that the evangelical resurgence may portend a religious revival in American life. Gallup notes the growing phenomenon of "turning within" on the part of many Christians who crave protection and security in a society convulsed with moral and social disintegration. For them material values no longer fulfill their deepest longings. Gallup credits the candid evangelical witness of President Jimmy Carter as giving credibility to this movement, a factor particularly important to young people who are searching for direction in a rudderless world.[10] The 1979 Gallup poll in *Christianity Today* revealed that more than one-third of the adult population in the United States have had a dramatic religious experience, eight out of ten of them believe Jesus Christ to be divine, sixty-five million adults believe the Bible is inerrant and half of them affirm that God created Adam and Eve to be the parents of the human race. Here Gallup predicts that the 1980s will be "the decade of the evangelicals." He notes that, in comparison to nonevangelicals, evangelicals give more in time and money to their churches, are more zealous in the expression of their faith, and are beginning to speak out more on social and political issues.[11]

To be sure, the evangelical resurgence of the 1970s has exhibited tremendous variety in its appeal to diverse individuals and groups in their search for meaning and security. The threads uniting these groups are thin and fragile. But what the new evangelicals have in common is not so much the several convictions stated earlier, but a belief in the

Lordship of Jesus Christ, the need for a personal conversion to him and a dependence on the Holy Scripture as testimony to God's will for our lives. Although some evangelicals remain fundamentalist in their insistence upon a literal interpretation of scripture, the 1970s witnessed the emergence of a new strain of evangelicals who believe that it is possible and appropriate to take less conservative theological and moral stands while still requiring a personal conversion. It is this strain that we are interested in pursuing here.

One example is Jack Rogers who declares in his book *Confessions of a Conservative Evangelical* (1974):

> To find freedom, wholeness, and involvement with the world does not mean rejecting the Christian faith. For me, it means acknowledging that I am becoming more critical of my conservatism. It means believing that I am emerging as more evangelical. . . . I want to say to Christians who are changing: It's OK—you can become less conservative and more evangelical.[12]

Rogers is a typical manifestation of the "New Evangelical" of the seventies. He was raised as a conservative Christian; he was told specifically what to believe and how to act, a stance reinforced in his college years. It was while he participated in a work camp project in Egypt that he first experienced culture shock and began to question the close identification that fundamentalism often made between the Christian faith and specific stereotypes in forms of expression, beliefs, and behavior. He came to see that the task of the Christian is to translate the basic teachings of the scripture with the aid of biblical scholarship into the thought categories of the present day. In making this translation Rogers believes that evangelicals can make significant changes in their understanding of traditional theological and ethical views. With respect to the former he insists, "Biblical scholars have long known that the first eleven chapters of Genesis are theological, not scientific, information."[13] With respect to the latter, he suggests, "The Bible commends no one style of life. It does not absolutize the way of life sanctioned by the majority in a culture—especially not when that culture is materialistic, individualistic, and selfish."[14]

Rogers typifies the major new thrust of the evangelicalism of the 1970s: a deep commitment to the God and Christ of the scriptures yet a willingness to be a citizen of the world and a desire to adopt the best of both. The fact that Rogers is professor of theology at Fuller Theological Seminary, a traditional stronghold of conservative religious views, indicates both the power and acceptance of the new evangelicalism. A position similar to Jack Rogers' emerged in George Ladd's groundbreaking book, *The New Testament and Criticism* (1967). Here Ladd maintained that evangelicals could no longer avoid the historical-critical method in their approach to scriptures:

> Since the Bible is the Word of God given in the words of men, an adequate study of the Bible demands what we have chosen to call a historical-theological methodology. . . . The author confessedly writes from a conservative or evangelical point of view, and believes that the Bible is itself the inspired Word of God, the only infallible rule for faith and practice. . . . His concern is, from this perspective, to illustrate to those who share his theological convictions that there is a critical method which is not hostile to this "high" view of the Bible, that, in fact, the Bible demands such critical study.[15]

As suggested above it would be impossible to give an adequate summary and interpretation of the multidimensional varieties of this religious phenomenon. One can only point to a few of the leaders, movements, and trends. Anyone who wishes to pursue this phase of American religion in greater depth should read the three books written by Richard Quebedeaux: *The Young Evangelicals* (1974), *The New Charismatics* (1976), and *The Worldly Evangelicals* (1978). A summary of his three books is in essence an overview of the new evangelicalism.

In his first book Quebedeaux points out that the secularism of the 1960s was not as widespread as its advocates proclaimed.

> Something is happening on the contemporary scene which indicates that modern man might not, in fact, be so utterly free of religious needs and aspirations as was hitherto supposed. The current rediscovery of the supernatural, the upsurge in popularity of Eastern relgious traditions and the occult, the renaissance of Evangelical and enthusiastic Christianity—affecting all strata of Western society—together point to the re-emergence of what Andrew Greeley calls "unsecular man."[16]

It is this "unsecular individual" who finds the New Evangelicalism so palatable, the individual who is yearning for a spiritual faith with deep historical roots, who yet needs to come to terms with contemporary culture. Protestant liberalism cannot fulfill this yearning since it denies the classical teachings of the Protestant Reformation. And Neo-Orthodoxy has failed in its refusal to accept the *words* of scripture as authoritative and in its downplay of the importance of the conversion experience.

For this reason two streams of orthodoxy have come to prominence in recent times: Fundamentalism and Evangelicalism. Fundamentalists range in belief from those political conservatives who are so sure of the truth of the literal teachings of the Bible that they separate themselves from all other people to await the imminent return of Jesus, to those who shun a close allegiance with political conservatism on the grounds that politics and religion should be kept separate. One important strain of Fundamentalism, particularly strong as we move into the 1980s, has failed to heed Richard Pierard's warning mentioned earlier and has linked its religious beliefs with equally conservative political convictions. As one example, evangelist Jerry Falwell's "moral majority" movement was exceedingly aggressive in the political campaigns of 1980. This well-financed pressure group held as its primary goal the defeat of any political candidate who had moderate views on disarmament, abortion, homosexuality, and pornography, and opposed prayer in the public schools.

The "New Evangelicals" are close to the mainstream of American society and form a definite alternative to the Protestant ecumenical movement on the one hand and Fundamentalism on the other. In the New Evangelicalism of recent date Quebedeaux observes more concern for the social dimensions and complexities of Christianity and less dependence on traditional forms of piety, more interest in the whole person and less in the conversion of souls, and more willingness to enter into dialogue with other Christian groups. These New Evangelicals are often less concerned with forming their own denomination of kindred spirits—the splinter groups that have appeared so often in the conservative wing of American religion—than with taking part in the already established denominations. They believe they are filling a spiritual gap apparent in these mainstream religious groups by their strong commitment to a biblical faith, their demand for a life-transforming conversion, and their advocacy of a definite and real purpose to life. Quebedeaux maintains:

In this respect, Billy Graham's cautious Evangelical reformism is far more appealing to the moderate stance of Middle America than either the activism of Harvey Cox's sometimes radical Liberalism or the reactionary conservatism of Carl MacIntire's Separate Fundamentalism.[17]

The revolution that has occurred in the evangelical movement in the 1970s has been summarized by Quebedeaux in four categories.

First, there is an interest in developing a richer understanding of the inspiration and authority of Scripture as the basis for action in the world. Second, it is felt that evangelism must always be the proclamation of the Gospel in its *entirety*—relevant to the whole man or woman and *all* his other needs. Third, there is a new emphasis on discipleship and on discovering values appropriate to the transformed life in Christ. And finally, it is believed that the institutional church should function corporately not only as the community of the saved but also as an instrument of reconciliation— calling alienated men and women to be reconciled to God, to one another, and to their own selves.[18]

Quebedeaux believes that as the New Evangelicals become more interested in an intellectual study of scripture, more involved in the world's social problems, and less hung up on outmoded prohibitions against certain forms of behavior—for example, drinking, dancing, etc.—and as the liberals become more Bible-centered and show a willingness to take their Christian discipleship more seriously, then there is reason to believe that evangelicals and liberals can find common cause.

In his second book, *The New Charismatics: The Origins, Development, and Significance of Neo-Pentecostalism,* Quebedeaux assesses the movement for charismatic renewal that has become so strong in the 1970s, concluding that

[Charismatic Renewal] rejects the rational evangelical god of the intellect— the great giver of propositional truth—in favor of the God you can feel, respond to and love, the God who *cares* about our present and our future. It is the knowledge of this God, given through the experience of his Holy Spirit, that binds Charismatics together. . . . In a word, Charismatic Renewal is a celebration in our generation that God has not forgotten his promises, that he is, in fact and deed, a living God, totally committed to work in *evidential* ways through the lives of those committed to him.[19]

Charismatic Renewal has its roots in the pentecostal movement which flourished at the beginning of this century. However, this newer manifestation is more a middle-class phenomenon, weak on doctrine and strong on personal faith, and finds most of its adherents in the major denominations whereas the earlier groups were of the lower socio-economic strata and formed and continue to maintain their own denominational structures. Quebedeaux states that, despite the great theological diversity among the charismatics, what they do have in common is their stress on the baptism of the Holy Spirit which results in a rebirth of their own personal lives. The charismatic movement emerged in the 1960s but did not become a major factor in the religious life until the 1970s; the Catholic charismatic movement originated only in 1967. Charismatics are often, but not always, marked by a stress on the gifts of healing and speaking in tongues, and more often than not lack a deep social conscience, affirming instead the values of their culture. A deep individual spiritual piety is their common trademark. Although this phenomenon of the 1970s is often excessive in its appeal to personal conversion and anti-intellectual in its concern for doctrine, it has been able to unite spiritually laity and clergy of most Christian groups to a degree unmatched by the institutional ecumenical movement.

Meanwhile, because of their disdain for doctrine and their appeal to experience charismatics are sharply divided about proper vehicles for such experience. The older Pentecostals usually belong to well-established right-wing denominations such as the Assemblies of God and Church of God. They put great emphasis on speaking in tongues. The modern charismatics belong for the most part to mainstream Protestant denominations and the Roman Catholic Church. Speaking in tongues is not as acceptable to their middle-class values; they stress spiritual vitality and exuberance. Moreover, the modern charismatics are often sharply divided among themselves, largely because their leaders frequently develop delusions of grandeur which they find difficult to share with other leaders with similar qualities. Perhaps the greatest indictment of the charismatic movement as a whole is that social problems become subordinate to the conversion experience.

In his latest book, *The Worldly Evangelicals,* a sequel to his *The Young Evangelicals,* Quebedeaux departs from his uncritical and optimistic attitude toward the evangelical left evident in his earlier study. He suggests ways in which evangelicals in recent years have adopted more and more the practices of their surrounding culture. He writes:

> Evangelicals today face the toughest of all religious problems: In what way or degree is Christ relevant to the situation in which the Christian must live? How can a follower of Jesus Christ be ''in the world but not of it''? This is the question of Christ and culture.[20]

For example, with respect to sexuality, Quebedeaux writes, ''In *The Young Evangelicals,* I suggested that evangelicals enjoy sex, too, but are afraid to admit it. Today, they shout it from the house tops.''[21] Concerning the Bible, evangelicals have moved away from the total inerrancy of scripture in all matters and are increasingly advocating limited inerrancy, maintaining that the Bible's authority on matters related to history and the cosmos is not necessarily accurate. Also, ''relational theology,'' stressing relationships among people following God's commandment to love, is becoming more important for some evangelicals than specific historical doctrines. Because the appeal of the Charismatic Renewal movement cuts across denominational and theological boundaries, it has served to push doctrinal issues into the background. Quebedeaux notes that evangelicals now find their theological insights in those neo-orthodox theologians condemned so vehemently by their predecessors of the 1950s and 1960s, thinkers such as Karl Barth, Emil Brunner, Dietrich Bonhoeffer, and Reinhold Niebuhr.

> The works of these theologians are studied and taught sympathetically in evangelical seminaries. Evangelical scholars are writing an ever increasing number of articles and books paying high tribute to them. . . . Neo-Orthodoxy, carried and nurtured by evangelical theology, may prove to be stronger and more durable.[22]

As a further example, the Intervarsity Christian Fellowship, the college student group that was once a bastion of biblical literalism and traditional codes of morality, has now in many places taken over the function of the mainline ecumenical campus ministries.

> There are no legalistic lifestyle expectations on IVCF staff and students. . . . Young Evangelicals drink . . . four-letter and other once-proscribed words are now common in the conversation of left evangelicals . . . [23]

Left-wing evangelicals are moving so far to the left in matters of faith and practice and in the priority they give to personal experience that one analyst, Robert S. Ellwood, questions whether the new evangelicalism is

> really something new *within* evangelicalism, or is [it] the shaky, searching first steps of a reborn liberalism? . . . I wonder if history were not repeating itself rather than doing something new . . . perhaps paralleling the well-known changes in rhetoric and style that evangelical churches like the Methodist underwent several generations ago as their constituencies moved up the education and affluence ladders.[24]

According to Quebedeaux, then, the new evangelicals have made a definite shift to the left. In an article entitled "The Evangelicals: New Trends and New Tensions" which he wrote in 1976, he summarizes this trend as follows:

> . . . evangelical theology is becoming more centrist, more open to biblical criticism and more accepting of science and broad cultural analysis. . . . [Their] evangelism looks more like the call to social justice and discipleship than the traditional call to conversion. One can even discern among them a subtle shift in the direction of belief in universal salvation. And some of the younger evangelicals, anyway, may be just about ready to celebrate the secular city. . . . Only time will tell to what degree all of this will eventually become pervasive. But one thing is certain. Evangelicalism will never be the same.[25]

One of the charges commonly leveled against the evangelical movement has been its over-emphasis on inward personal piety with a consequent minimal concern for social issues. A mark of the New Evangelicalism has been a deepened commitment to the social dimension of the Christian gospel. Noted evangelical theologian Harold Ockenga points to this trend.

> The new evangelicalism concerns itself not only with personal salvation, doctrinal truth and an eternal point of reference, but also with the problems of race, of war, of class struggle, of liquor control, of juvenile delinquency, of immorality, and of national imperialsim. . . . The new evangelicalism believes that orthodox Christians cannot abdicate their responsibility in the social scene.[26]

A turning-point occurred in November of 1973 when over forty leading evangelicals met in Chicago to discuss the proper relationship between their faith and world issues. Out of that meeting came A Declaration of Evangelical Social Concern which stated in part:

> We acknowledge that God requires justice. But we have not proclaimed or demonstrated his justice to an unjust American society. Although the Lord calls us to defend the social and economic rights of the poor and the oppressed, we have mostly remained silent. We deplore the historic involvement of the church in America with racism and the conspicuous responsibility of the evangelical community for perpetuating the personal attitudes and institutional structures that have divided the body of Christ along color lines. . . . So we call our fellow evangelical Christians to demonstrate repentance in a Christian discipleship that confronts the social and political injustice of our nation. . . . We make this declaration in the biblical hope that Christ is coming to consummate the Kingdom, and we accept this claim on our total discipleship till he comes.[27]

This declaration was deliberately aimed at the evangelical Protestants. In the words of evangelical theologian John Howard Yoder, a conference participant, this declaration is showing for Evangelicalism "the signs of a new openness to prophetic social critique, however unwelcome the resulting concrete social judgments will be in the heartland."[28]

One significant movement on the evangelical left is the People's Christian Coalition, begun in 1971, with its headquarters now in Washington, D.C. Under the leadership of Jim Wallis, this fifty-member community publishes the monthly magazine, *Sojourners,* which is in essence a biblically sophisticated evangelical appeal for peace and justice. Its articles are for the most part hard-hitting radical attacks against militarism, racism, sexism, and other social ills caused by capitalist oppression in the United States. Its regular contributors include evangelicals Clark Pinnock, John Howard Yoder, John R. W. Stott, and Senator Mark O. Hatfield. Recently *Sojourners* has begun to recommend literature relating faith to social action. The book list reads like a bibliography for liberation, black, and feminist theologians.

At this point some discussion of the ideas of some evangelical theologians who have published important recent works should clarify the above sketch of the New Evangelicalism of the 1970s. John Yoder's *The Politics of Jesus* (1972) is a vigorous affirmation of the pacifism of Jesus based on the Gospel of Luke. Yoder argues that Jesus' pacifism is normative for a contemporary Christian ethic.

> A social style characterized by the creation of a new community and the rejection of violence of any kind is the theme of New Testament proclamation from beginning to end, from right to left. The cross of Christ is a model of Christian social efficacy, the power of God for those who believe.[29]

Indefatigable Carl Henry is now writing a four-volume tome on the general theme *God, Revelation, and Authority*. His avowed goal is to provide evangelical theology with a solid intellectual basis. Henry vigorously opposes the extremes of the evangelical movement which overstress immediate personal experience to the exclusion of intellectual substance.

> The Christian revelation contends that the meaning of the cosmos and man and history is transcendentally given in the form of intelligible divine disclosure. On this basis Christianity professes to supply the enduring conceptuality that alone makes possible an ongoing unity of theology, philosophy, history, and science. . . . Some may say that tests of revelation or truth are highly inappropriate, and that human creatures ought to accept the divine without question. But tests of truth are wholly appropriate.[30]

Henry argues for a view of scripture as essentially a set of truths that can be known through reason. Since God is the author of these truths and truth is known only through human perception, Henry argues for the "propositional errorlessness" of scripture. But he admits that there are passages in the Bible which he cannot explain.

Jack Rogers' edited book *Biblical Authority* (1977) consists of a series of essays by leading evangelical scholars which indicate that even if one accepts scripture as the basis of authority, as evangelicals do, there is wide disagreement on how to interpret that authority. In the words of David Hubbard, president of Fuller Theological Seminary:

> To revere the Word is admirable; it is, however, no substitute for using every possible—every God-given means—for understanding it. Reading literal meanings where they were not intended or spiritual meanings where they are not present or forcing harmonizations where they were not intended is just as dishonoring to the Bible as failing to hear its intended spiritual message.[31]

In his later book *The Authority and Interpretation of the Bible* (1979), coauthored with Donald McKirn, Rogers seeks for a middle view between subjectivism and rationalism.

Like Carl Henry, Donald Bloesch wants to give conceptual credibility to evangelicalism. In his book *The Evangelical Renaissance* (1973) he warns evangelicals against an obscurantism that refuses to accept the legitimate contributions of historical criticism and calls Karl Barth the most profound Christian theologian of our age. In his major work, *Essentials of Evangelical Theology* (1978), he disputes the popular view that Evangelicalism signifies a particular kind of religious experience rather than a doctrinal basis. He insists that experience and doctrine are mutually essential. Bloesch is critical of what he terms the "ghetto mentality" of some strains of contemporary Evangelicalism which inhibits creative contributions in the area of systematic theology. He objects to those popular evangelicals who "seek a continuous mountain-top experience and avoid controversial theological issues."[32] In his second volume (1979) Bloesch amplifies this point, suggesting that the main reason why Evangelicalism suffers from theological poverty is that intellectual accomplishments are considered far less significant than the winning of souls.[33]

Bloesch's criticism is important. A huge number of pop-evangelical books are pouring from the presses consisting of personal testimonies to mountain-top experiences to the exclusion of intellectual rigor. Such books make for easy reading and thus large sales. Many evangelicals are finding it difficult to treat the narrow road between overweening piety and arid intellectual respectability. Some writers are trying to bridge this difficult gap. Examples are Keith Miller (*The Taste of New Wine, A Second Touch, Habitation of Dragons, The Edge of Adventure* coauthored with Bruce Larson, *Please Love Me*) and Tom Skinner (*How Black Is the Gospel?, Words of Revolution*, and *If Christ Is the Answer, What Are the Questions?*).

The reservations and qualifications expressed by Henry and Bloesch are rendered even more significant in the light of the recent explosion of television evangelism, using all the latest slick techniques of Madison Avenue. This modern retailing of evangelical Christianity enters the living rooms of millions of Americans with semi-disco hymnody and pre-packaged words of comfort ("God loves you; He really does."). This type of presentation, so insulting to any thoughtful Christian, is proving to be a considerable embarrassment to evangelical theologians who realize that evangelicalism needs intellectual credibility and can only be harmed by naive buffoonery.

Another thorn in the flesh for the New Evangelicals is the small though vocal group of conservative Christians who have become disenchanted with the lack of tradition and formal ceremony among the born-again Christians for whom the immediate experience of Christ constitutes the focal point of faith. These disillusioned evangelicals, in their yearning for ritual and historical roots, have found common cause with right-wing Episcopalians in their mutual need to combine religious fervor with anti-modernist theological and liturgical beliefs and practices. Their forum is the *New Oxford Review,* a monthly publication that has as its goal the marriage of orthodox tradition with evangelical exuberance.

The New Evangelicalism of the 1970s, then, covers a wide spectrum of views. Its main feature has been a move to the left and into the mainstream of biblical and theological scholarship. In so doing its proponents have alienated the right-wing evangelicals who remain committed to an uncritical biblical inerrancy. The Evangelical Theological Society was founded in 1949 by right-wing theologians to counteract the turn to the left by some of their colleagues. But the move to the left has been essential, for, as Carl Henry has asserted, "Those who declare [that] the unabashed commitment to biblical inerrancy guarantees theological vitality have the past twenty-five years of meager production by the Evangelical Theological Society to explain."[34] James Barr makes this same point in his book *Fundamentalism.*

> Though much solid and valuable work is carried out by biblical scholars who are also conservatives, much or most of this is actually in conflict with the fundamentalist doctrinal principles and can be taken to support them only through misrepresentation or misunderstanding. It is of course perfectly possible that conservative evangelicals might produce a set of intellectual arguments that would seriously disturb mainstream theology and biblical study; but they would have to be arguments quite other than those which have now been standard for about a century.[35]

As the New Evangelicals have moved to the left, they have entered into dialogue with black, liberation, and feminist theologians. Indeed, James Barr insists that

> A single social movement such as modern feminism, once it attained to serious influence, seems to have done more to alter conservative evangelicalism than all the works of scholars and theologians.[36]

It is important that evangelicals recognize the "outer history" they share with other believers and theological movements. But in this more into the mainstream of academic scholarship the New Evangelicals have lost something of their distinctiveness, a factor reinforced as they have become more a part of the mainline Protestant denominations. Richard Quebedeaux has called attention to their present affinity for Neo-Orthodox theologians. As suggested above, Robert Ellwood wonders whether the New Evangelicalism is the vanguard of a reborn liberalism. And Martin Marty warns:

> . . . evangelicalism is taking on and will increasingly take on the burdens of interpretation and accommodation that have created numerous troubles for the mainstream groups. . . . They cannot expect a serene life as they try to remain a "cognitive minority" while they have become a kind of social behavioral majority far beyond the borders of middle America.[37]

The major problem for the New Evangelicalism today is an age-old one. how does one remain unswerving in one's loyalty to the Christian faith and yet at the same time live with integrity in the modern world? In his book *Evangelicals in Search of Identity* (1976) Carl Henry bemoans the infighting among evangelicals, their lack of interest in serious theological literature, and their failure to seek a truly biblical ecumenism with a united involvement in political, social, and economic concerns. He pleads for "a recovery of the larger sense of evangelical family in which fellow-believers recognize their common answerability to God in his scripturally given Word and their responsibility for and to each other within the body of faith."[38] To find common cause with a Christian faith that is "in but not of the world" will be the primary issue for the New Evangelicals in the decade of the eighties.

7
Roman Catholic Theology

During the late 1960s there emerged in North America a strain of Roman Catholic secular theology activated by the reforms of the Second Vatican Council which inaugurated a radical transformation within the Roman Catholic church on this continent. The seeds of secular theology had been planted as early as the nineteenth century in the Catholic modernist movement. Yet out of the unique historical climate produced by Vatican II and the simultaneous crisis in American Protestant theology caused by the death-of-God theology of the middle 1960s there appeared a breed of secular Catholic theism which transformed the future of Catholic theology.

By the 1960s the Catholic church in America was finally in a position to surmount some of the handicaps caused by its long history of preoccupation with questions of American Catholic acculturation. Vatical II proved to be a stimulus to Catholic theology both for North Americans present at the council and for those responding to conciliar statements back home. The spirit in which Pope John XXIII opened the Council provided encouragement to American Catholic theologians to abandon their wariness toward change and become involved in the renewal of the Church. The following excerpt from Pope John's opening address indicates a changed mentality in the church.

> In the present order of things, Divine Providence is leading us to a new order of human relations which, by men's own efforts and even beyond their very expectations, are directed toward the fulfillment of God's superior and inscrutable designs. And everything, even human differences, leads to the greater good of the Church . . . [1]

It is important to note that the Catholic church in America faced a very different kind of crisis than American Protestants confronted in, notably, the death-of-God theology. The problems Catholics faced during the mid-1960s were of a more external, less fundamental nature than those raised by the death-of-God theologians. Nevertheless, there is evidence of Catholic awareness of the crisis in Christianity professed by Altizer, Hamilton, and van Buren and its implications for American Catholicism. One example of this is a series of lectures entitled "The Problem of God—Yesterday and Today" delivered at Yale in 1962 by the prominent American Jesuit theologian John Courtney Murray.[2] In these lectures delivered during the initial stages of the death-of-God controversy Murray addresses the universal problem of God as particularly timely for contemporary Christians. Murray approaches the problem in a manner similar to that of Protestant theologian Gabriel Vahanian: God exists, but the godless person is incapable of faith in God. Thus, faced with modern affirmations of godlessness, Murray does not conclude that God is dead. He maintains that the transcendent God of Christianity can enter human experience and liberate the believer from one's own sense of being without god.

Six years later, in 1968, when the death-of-God theology was already beyond its prime, another American Jesuit, Avery Dulles, addressed the death-of-God theology itself in a book entitled *Revelation and the Quest for Unity*. Dulles reviews the theologies of Hamilton, Altizer, and van Buren, citing these as symptomatic of the attitudes underlying modern human existence. Such attitudes include the dissatisfaction with and distrust of traditional metaphysical religious answers, a preoccupation with practical answers, and an intense concern for human freedom. Dulles suggests that the death-of-God issue can help believing Christians to clarify in their own minds what it means to bear witness to Christ as God.

> Perhaps the best answer to the "death of god" theologians was given by the second century Jewish rabbi Simon Bar Yochai, who summed up much of what I have tried to say in a challenging sentence which he placed in the mouth of God: "If you are my witness, I am God, and if you are not my witness I am, so to speak, no longer God.[3]

Aside from the attempts of American Jesuits Murray and Dulles to deal with the God problem, two more creative treatments of the concerns of death-of-God theologians were produced by the Dutch Catholic theologians Edward Schillebeeckx and Robert Adolfs, both of whom visited America on lecture tours during 1967. Each produced an assessment of Protestant radical theology in America from the perspective of the post-Vatican II Catholic church. Schillebeeckx deals with the death-of-God theology in a book entitled *God, The Future of Man* (1968).[4] He locates the roots of the present crisis in Christian belief in the traditional separation of the god-concept from human experience and suggests that silence becomes a new way to speak about God, that is, silence which can express one's faith in God as it is shown in concern for one's neighbors in the secular world. He tries to combine an awareness of God's presence in the modern world with a belief in a vital, dynamic divine transcendence.

Robert Adolfs discusses the death of God in his book *The Grave of God* (1967). The fact that the grave turns out to be the Catholic church illustrates an important element of Catholic renewal in the 1960s with its overriding concern for the transformation of the Church. Reform in the Catholic context did not mean replacing old structures but renovating those already standing. Therefore, Adolfs does not emulate the death-of-God theologians. Their tragic flaw is that, "They have greeted secularization with altogether too much enthusiasm and too few reservations."[5] Adolfs advocates the purging of the authority structures of the Church on its way to realizating the goal of becoming the "People of God." Without this transformation the Church will become the grave of God.

> If the Church continues to do what she is now doing and to be what she is now, then she has no future. Her fine churches and beautiful cathedrals will become the sepulchral monuments, the graves of God and of Christianity.[6]

The ways in which Murray, Dulles, Schillebeeckx, and Adolfs deal with the problem of God leaves one with at least a partial view of the concerns of the Catholic church in America during the 1960s. Although they acknowledge the symptoms of godlessness in the modern world, none of these Catholic theologians rejects the reality of a transcendent God. For them, the Christian God in divine *transcendence* provides the only hope for modern Christianity in its present crisis. Yet all four men admit a need for theological renewal within the ecclesiastical framework. The Second Vatican Council provided a timely opportunity for the Catholic church as an institution to see itself in a new light, as an "open Church," the "People of God." This change in self-understanding or consciousness made possible the new radical questioning in

Catholic theology which began late in the 1960s and continues into the present.

With the late 1960s came increasing confusion and discontent within the American church focusing on the questions of liturgical experimentation, clerical celibacy, and contraception. This was intensified by the appearance of the papal encyclical *Humanae Vitae* (On Human Life) which reaffirmed the Catholic ban on artificial birth control. Catholic sociologist Andrew Greeley judges this encyclical to have been "one of the worst mistakes in the history of Catholic Christianity."[7] *Humanae Vitae* stimulated both extreme turmoil and polarization within the Catholic church. This tension, in combination with the post-conciliar stress on ecumenical acceptance of the beliefs affirmed by other Christian churches, ultimately made necessary the acceptance of a greater pluralism within American Catholicism.

Thus a new phase begins in the renewal of the Church which is a theological reconstruction from inside out, a recasting of the Christian faith in accordance with the changing forms of the Church. It is during this phase that post-conciliar Catholics seek to deal with the more basic theological questions. Although Protestant radical theology, as we have noted, had already begun to lose its punch by the end of the 1960s, this new form of Catholic theology arises in part out of the ashes of the death of God. By the beginning of the 1970s Roman Catholics Leslie Dewart, Gregory Baum, Avery Dulles, and the European Hans Küng are already involved in a theological renewal in which they discuss the very meaning of God and Christian belief. Although, to be sure, many other Catholic theologians are also opting for radical theological revision during this period, we shall concentrate our attention on the four mentioned above.

When Dewart, Baum, Dulles, and Küng ask the meaning of God, they do not ask if God is in fact dead, but rather in what way *does God exist* in contemporary secular experience and especially in the life of the modern church community. Like Bishop Robinson in *Honest to God,* all four theologians attempt to move beyond a God metaphysically "out there" to one who is within human experience, affirming the transcendent nature of God but stressing God's immanence. In seeking to preserve divine transcendence and the unity of the Church, they depart from the sort of radicalism expressed in the death-of-God theology to express a more reluctant radicalism like that of Bishop Robinson.

LESLIE DEWART

The thought of Leslie Dewart expressed in *The Future of Belief* (1966) and *The Foundations of Belief* (1966) contributed greatly to a shift in North American Catholic theology from a preoccupation with the question of the Church to one with the question of God. In both of his books Dewart addresses two related questions constituting essentially the same inquiry:

> . . . Can the Christian faith be deemed truly to develop and unequivocally to evolve . . . even if it is assumed that this faith is *supernatural* and that its object is *revealed?* . . . [and] . . . Can the Christian faith be said truly to develop and unequivocally to evolve, on the assumption that this faith is true and that its object is real?[8]

Dewart is questioning the meaning and authority of belief in the Christian God in the light of the present "consciousness" of the modern seeker. And both questions spring from the common presupposition that, "It is contemporary experience *as a whole* that is incongruous with Christian belief *as a whole.*"[9]

Dewart's view of the human being as an evolving entity with a changed and changing consciousness, as the individual "come of age" or coming of age, is central to his theology. Dewart sees the evolution of belief, the development of dogma, as an implication of the vital factor of human experience in any form of Christian faith. And the development or reorientation of the central concept of God becomes necessary in Dewart's theology not merely as a way of following the development of dogma to its fullest implications. Rather, Dewart asserts:

> . . . the integration of Christian belief and contemporary experience must logically begin—that is, cannot in the end abstract from—the integration of the *concept of God* with contemporary experience.[10]

With this central concern in mind Leslie Dewart proposes his theological realignments designed to take place within the framework of the Church. For Dewart, Christian belief implicitly includes the historical and social dimensions of the believer's experience; and the Church, also historically and socially conditioned, becomes the site of a dynamic evolution of belief.[11] However, Dewart in no way implies the limitation of God to these human dimensions; divine transcendence is still very much a part of his theology.

In line with this view of Christian belief as necessarily contingent upon human variables is Dewart's proposal for theological renewal through the "dehellenization of dogma." This is necessary because he views early Christianity as having been "hellenized" by an early exposure to Greek metaphysical thought, at which time the ideals of immutability, stability, and impassibility were introduced into the Christian conceptual framework. This drastically shaped its way of speaking about God, as these characteristics came to be seen as the attributes of God as well as requirements for dogmatic statements affirming belief in God. Because Christianity became hellenized down to its very foundations, Dewart's task of dehellenization constitutes a radical theological reconstruction within the Catholic church.

Dewart's proposed dehellenization refers to the removal of the remnants of Greek experience, once legitimate expressions of Christian theistic belief during a certain early period in the development of the Church but which are now entrenched in static formulations of dogma without links to contemporary experience. The problem prompting the need for dehellenization arose as the secular experience of Christian belief began to depart from that of the hellenistic Christians. Today this departure is virtually complete and new concepts from modern experience must replace such hellenistic elements of faith as the conception of God as Being, and the idea of faith as rational knowledge of certain truths about a strictly supernatural God. Dewart's proposal for dehellenization means transcending traditional metaphysical expressions of belief to engage in what Dewart calls "meta-metaphysics." By meta-metaphysics Dewart means an investigation of the reality underlying even the metaphysical foundations of belief after the influence of Greek experience upon these forms has been separated and discarded. This has a positive side and a hopeful purpose, that is:

> . . . the conscious creation of the future of Christian belief . . . ideally through the invention of its own concepts and other forms of experience on the basis of an imaginative creative evolutionary leap ahead.[12]

Because of the static nature of the Christian theology operating under hellenistic principles, Dewart calls today's Christian theism "underdeveloped," "absolute theism." He prefers a growing, evolving, self-questioning "relative theism" engaged in an endless process of reorientation to human experience in the changing secular situation.

Dewart sees faith as a natural consequence of one's developing experience and evolution and conceives of no point at which one would not tend toward God, no matter how extensive the evolution of one's consciousness. Thus Dewart considers faith to be the transcendent dimension in human experience. This stands out in marked contrast to the traditional view of faith as the acknowledgment of truths beyond human consciousness. And this critical union between faith in God and human consciousness and experience also pervades Dewart's concept of revelation; he maintains that ''God can be seen to reveal himself to man, insofar as his presence to man affects decisively the individual and collective evolutionary history of human consciousness.''[13]

At the end of *The Future of Belief* Leslie Dewart illustrates his concept of relative theism by presenting five tentative proposals for the future realignment of the concept of God. It is interesting that Dewart's suggestions on this problem assume a negative form; they designate ways in which God will *not* be seen by future Christians. First, God may no longer be seen as a being or even as Being itself. This does not mean that from the human perspective there will no longer be a God, that deity will be nothing. Rather, God will be viewed as beyond all being, transcending it.

Second, Dewart considers it unlikely that future Christians will conceive of God as a person or even as a trinity of persons. Although he sees the concept of person as an acceptable metaphor, it is possibly due to the priority of human experience and existence in Dewart's theology that he is very sensitive to the inaccuracy of the term even in expressing what is metaphorically intended by the word *person*. Dewart maintains:

> . . . that God is, rather than a center of being to which we are drawn, an expansive force which impels persons to go out from and beyond themselves. The expression represents an effort, born out of an understandable impatience, to transcend the primitive God-being, God-person and God-object of absolute theism.[14]

Third, the so-called divine attributes (for example, omnipotence, eternity, immateriality, infinity, immutability, etc.) will be dealt with in a different manner by future Catholic theologians. Dewart uses the example of divine omnipotence, asserting that Christians will no longer be concerned with what it means to say that God has the power to do all things. Instead, the dynamic relationship between God and humanity should be stressed, so that omnipotence comes to be seen as "a radical openness of history."[15] Such a transformation of the concept of omnipotence should, according to Dewart, awaken Christians to a greater awareness of their responsibility to perform God's will in the world.

In like manner Dewart deals with God's eternity. The stress traditionally placed on God's lying beyond human history has, in Dewart's view, obscured the meaning of divine immanence and of the God-person relationship which must take place within the historical realm in which one lives one's Christian life. The human being as an historical creature can never really separate God from the medium of history in which humans experience God. According to Dewart, a change of emphasis is necessary—from the focus on God's eternity and God's ascendence over the submissive person, to a greater awareness of God as dynamic "presence" in the experience of the faithful.

Finally, Dewart states that God will not be considered supernatural by future Christians. He suggests that we should abandon the traditional distinction between the natural and the supernatural which he sees as introduced by the scholastics for apologetic purposes. Dewart finds the view of nature implied by such a distinction to be inconsistent with modern human experience. For Dewart, human nature is defined by one's relatedness to the divine. Further, "Grace is a historical fact; it is the irruption of God into man's history. Rather, it is the emergence of human history within the reality of God."[16]

Dewart asserts that the same name *God* should not be used for the presumably changed God-concept of the future. He does not attempt to suggest a new name which might also become meaningless in time as human consciousness evolves further. Instead, Dewart suggests that Christians attempt to speak about God without insisting upon a name: Christians should "reserve a special place for silence in discourse about God."[17] This suggestion is close to that made by Robinson a few years earlier and anticipates Schillebeeckx's proposal for silence in speaking about God in *God, the Future of Man* (1967).

GREGORY BAUM

Gregory Baum proposes a refocusing of theology which, like Dewart's, is based on the evolving experience of humanity and the resulting inadequacy of traditional dogmatic expressions of the Catholic faith. In three of his works in particular, *The Credibility of the Church Today* (1968), *Faith and Doctrine* (1969), and *Man Becoming* (1970), Baum outlines his theology, affirming the central importance of God's involvement in the process of human self-creation. This entails a divine immanence in theology similar to that proposed by Dewart which supplies in Baum's theology a sort of missing link between the faith expressed in scripture and tradition and that experienced in the secular life of Catholics today.

Central to Gregory Baum's theology is his concept of a gradual "doctrinal shift" within Catholic belief developing since the time of Maurice Blondel, a turn-of-the-century Roman Catholic philosopher. This shift, basically revolving around a belief in God's redemptive involvement in history, culminated in certain statements to this effect within the conciliar documents at Vatican II. Yet it is most significant that for Baum this shift itself originated in the experiences of the faithful, their beliefs, doubts, and problems as the Church responded to the confrontation of theology and the secular world. The shift, then, was not promulgated at Vatican II, nor was it an original contribution of Blondel. Rather, it was an acknowledgment of the implications of secular life for Catholic faith expressed in Blondel and surfacing in certain new ideas arising in the conciliar debates.

Along with this developing doctrinal shift, Baum sees an accompanying shift in the focus of the gospel in which it is becoming increasingly oriented toward the concerns of secular life. This has produced a new self-understanding on the part of the Church which has begun to acknowledge the importance of human consciousness in one's experience of God in the contemporary setting. In *The Credibility of the Church Today* Baum describes this new self-awareness in the term "Open Church," referring to the way in which the Church was engaged in a refocusing of the gospel around human experience, which paved the way for Baum's (and Dewart's) new theological emphases on change, progress, and human "becoming."

It is in relation to the term "becoming" that Baum acknowledges the debt of modern attempts at Catholic theological renewal to the thought of Maurice Blondel. A central concern in Blondel's writings is the idea of a continual process of personal human growth within human experience extending beyond the limits of human finitude almost to the "threshold" of the transcendent. This experience of faith as evolution and self-transcendence is what Blondel called "threshold apologetics." And in line with this view of the human relationship to God Blondel adopts his "method of immanence" which entails a rejection of "extrinsicist" notions about God as outsider, God as Wholly Other. Instead, Blondel views truth as present in human actions.

Baum's anthropology is implicitly a theological anthropology based upon a conviction similar to that of Blondel, namely that transcendence itself provides the structure for human action. Baum believes that the individual must make a crucial decision for or against faith and must choose "becoming" through involvement with transcendence. This option Daum calls "humanization," reminiscent of Vatican II language about a "new humanity." Therefore, the person of faith in Baum's view is one who listens, who becomes, and who acts, rather than one who knows and accepts absolute truths. The individual as a Christian needs dialogue and community to become more human.

Here Baum considers one's choice to become more human—to relate in community to the rest of humanity—to be a prerequisite to one's living in faith. The freedom with which the individual opts for becoming is nothing less than God's grace. This process of becoming, ever unfinished, is itself faith and involves God's saving activity. This does not entail the acceptance of a new knowledge, but rather a transformation of human consciousness, a radical self-awareness caused by the transcendent dimension one chooses in opting to become oneself.

Further, for Baum one's becoming involves more than one's acknowledgement of God's existence; it requires the person's engagement with this God in a living relationship. This is apparent in the following statement made by Baum.

> . . . What counts, ultimately, is man's engagement in life. Why? Because man who reaches out for what is true and holy, whatever his theoretical statements about reality, is in fact under the influence of divine grace. In this context, the conciliar text acknowledges what some authors call "secular grace."[18]

Still, Baum points to one problem which remains even after the gospel begins to be refocused, this being the inherent tension between faith as an abiding reality and its involvement in human experience which subjects it to the contingency and transience of the human situation. Yet this is no serious problem if dogmatic expressions are seen to evolve in order to ensure the abiding character of faith and the authenticity of the God-person relationship in a given place and time. Baum stresses the necessary distinction that the individual must make between divine reality and experience-oriented expressions of faith; the former never changes and the latter must shift as the focus of the gospel alters in the light of one's changing consciousness.

This element of doubt plays an important role in Baum's view of faith. Doubt becomes a dynamic force in the life of the church which constantly provides the possibility for doctrinal evolution. Thus, Baum rejects the traditional Catholic identification of doubt with unbelief. Instead, he sees doubt as a constant within faith—a crucial and abiding test of Church doctrine and a standard of experience by which Christians must check their beliefs in the forms that these assume both in the individual and in the communal worship of the Church. In this conviction of Baum's lies at least one reason why he considers it necessary to refocus even the concept of God. For Baum, ". . . to live with an unanswered question can be more in line with divine faith than to cling frantically to an answer which no longer satisfies our critical spirit."[19]

Gregory Baum's view of faith as described above springs from his phenomenological approach to theology which entails an examination of religious elements in ordinary experience and a conscious rejection of the totally unexperienceable "extrinsicist" forms of Christian metaphysics. Baum maintains that God's redemptive involvement in one's becoming takes place within one's most secular experiences. He proposes that ". . . there is a sort of empirical basis for theological reflection . . . that ordinary experience is not ordinary at all."[20]

The radical nature of Baum's departure from the theological position of the preconciliar church can be perceived in his stress on the continuity between the Christian doctrines of revelation and divine immanence. Thus, the element of distance between God and the individual and the possibility of drawing clear-cut distinctions between them are minimized in Baum's theology. His interpretation of both immanence and revelation revolve around the centrality of human experience, rather than reason, to Christian faith. Here revelation is God's disclosure in human experience not of truths about divine nature, but of God's very Self acting in the process of one's becoming.

Baum's view of faith as one's becoming, his attempt to reinstate the doctrine of divine immanence to its proper position in the life of the contemporary Church, and his interpretation of the experience of human doubt as a creative force within faith itself all converge in the two principles Baum sets forth in *Man Becoming*, designed to reinterpret the concept of God in the light of the experience of modern believers. The fact that the title of Baum's book on God in secular experience is *Man Becoming* aptly summarizes Baum's theology and these two principles. The first principle is that "there is no human standpoint from which God is simply man's over against."[21] The second follows logically: "Every sentence about God can be translated into a declaration about human life."[22]

Both of the above principles, especially the second one, expose a humanistic dimension of theology which would have been alien and probably suspect before the refocusing of the gospel had reached the stage it did at Vatican II. However, when one views Baum's two principles in their proper context—in relation to this experience-oriented view of faith and revelation, to his affirmation of both immanence and transcendence, and to the doctrinal shift which he sees to have culminated at Vatican II—then this apparent humanism does not seem to threaten the transcendence he affirms. Indeed, Baum sees a certain kind of humanism as integral to theology. He maintains, "It is revealed to us in Jesus that the human is the locus of the divine." Baum views such humanism as a dynamic element of Christianity, calling this theological stance "christological humanism."[23]

Also, in connection with his two principles Baum asserts that the need to reinterpret God is by no means a problem created by theologians. They are not merely rearranging the language of theology because, for example, it may have become too faimiliar to the individual, thus losing some of its original profound meaning. The problem lies deeper than that. Like Dewart, Baum sees human consciousness as evolving and one's experience of God in faith as colored by one's consciousness. Thus, the task of the theologian, exhibited in Baum's two principles for reinterpreting God, is that of reconceptualizing God out of the contemporary human consciousness.

AVERY DULLES

Avery Dulles proposes a third form of experience-oriented Christianity for Catholics in the 1970s in two of his recent works, *The*

Survival of Dogma (1973) and *Models of the Church* (1974). Dulles, like Dewart and Baum, attempts a "revitalization" of the most basic categories of traditional Catholic theology in light of the changed existence of the human being in the contemporary secular world. Dulles suggests a new view of one's experience of faith and revelation and treats the question of dogmatic development extensively. Yet he stops short of an attempt to reformulate the concept of God although it is seemingly implied by the other steps he takes to realign theology and the secular. He is more conservative than Dewart and Baum. In this way Dulles provides a good example of the pluralism within the theological renewal taking place in the Catholic church in North America.

In the introduction to *The Survival of Dogma* Avery Dulles describes the present crisis in Catholic theology. According to Dulles:

> . . . terms such as "faith," "authority" and "dogma"—to which one might add others, such as "revelation," "tradition," "doctrine," and "law"— have been too statically conceived. . . . All of these classical concepts can be revitalized if they are newly thought out against the background of a more flexible and processive world view.[24]

Here Dulles takes a stand close to that of Dewart in his proposals for the dehellenization of dogma. It is more than a translation of static concepts taken from earlier experiences of Christians in the Church which is being proposed here. Instead, it is the reconceptualization of certain fundamental elements of Christian experience in the light of our contemporary consciousness which is suggested by Dulles.

Faith for Dulles is also historical, subject to changes in cultural and social situations; in fact, he sees faith as necessarily flexible—having the potential to change with the experience of the believers—if it is to be faith at all. Dulles's view of the social and historical dimensions of faith, which posit its necessary development, is similar to that of Dewart and Baum. Yet Dulles places a stronger emphasis than the other two on the influence of historical forms and expressions of faith upon the experience of Christians today. Because of this, renewal in theology becomes a more complex, less "radical" task for Dulles. This might explain why he does not carry his revitalizing all the way to the concept of God. Dulles asserts, "Paradoxically, faith must move back in order to move forward; it never loses contact with its own previous history."[25]

In his book *Models of the Church* Dulles applies the conviction that the historical forms of Christian expressions of faith influence the contemporary experience of Christian belief. He proposes "models" of the Church to suggest ways in which the Church can become a more vital concept in the consciousness of the faithful today, playing a more dynamic role in their experience of faith. Dulles notes that during the past few decades American Catholics have experienced an unprecedented acceleration in shifting from one model to another. He suggests five models that are held—in varying degrees—by Catholic believers today. Dulles admits that his choice of five models is somewhat arbitrary. Yet his point in choosing this particular methodology is that the theological pluralism prevalent in the post-conciliar Church provides a situation in which theologian and believer must be willing to refer to several models or sets of models of the Church simultaneously, at the same time exercising the responsibility of differentiating which aspects of each model are appropriate expressions of the faith in one's particular experience. Since each model implies a different emphasis in theology, christology, faith, and dogma, Dulles's proposal that we relate to all of them in varying degrees simultaneously represents the complex, subjective, pluralistic theological task that he envisions for Catholics in America in the 1970s.

Briefly, the basic distinctions between Dulles's five models are as follows. The model of the Catholic church as institution stresses its role as a structural, political society. This model aptly describes the self-awareness of the Church hierarchy of the late nineteenth century and includes a hierarchical conception of the Church as a divinely ordained authority over all aspects of human life. The second model, the Church as mystical communion, is described by such biblical images of the Church as Body of Christ and, more recently, as People of God. Here the Church is viewed as an internally cohesive community (not a political union) of individuals bound together by creeds, worship, the sacraments, and fellowship. Dulles presents a third model, the Church as sacrament, in some sense a synthesis of the first two. Here the Church becomes a visible sign of God's redemptive grace as well as the dispenser and the event of this grace in the community of the Church. The Church in the fourth model is the herald of the Word of God. Here the Word is of primary importance and sacraments are secondary. This is a kerygmatic model that betrays the influence of Karl Barth within the

Catholic theology of this century. Finally, the model of the Church as Servant emphasizes the role of the Church as a part of the modern world. Dulles finds this model to be the most appropriate to secular theology and ecomenical dialogue in the Church today. For it conceives of the Church as having a mission within the world and as evolving with the consciousness of the modern believer, so that it can continue to address itself to the Christian experience of God in the changing world.

In *Models of the Church* Dulles also makes certain general predictions about the theology of the future. He anticipates greater modernization of its structures, increased engagement in ecumenical activity, and even more internal pluralism within the Church. Avery Dulles' use of "models" of the Church exemplifies his central concern for faith as the experience of members of the Church community, his realization of the need for change in the Church during periods of transition, and his sense of the flexibility and pluralism necessary within the faith of the Catholic church.

In summary, Dulles asserts that the only possible way for faith to retain its meaning lies with its flexibility, its ability to alter its exterior form each time the cultural experience of believers adjusts radically. For Dulles, the static conception of faith characterized by precounciliar metaphysically-based theology eliminated the true basis of faith—the human "existential confrontation" with the divine. Preservation of flexibility and pluralism within the church with regard to dogma should render Christian communities open to the experience of confrontation with transcendent reality in Christ, as this is naturally available to the individual in secular experience.

The above attempts of Leslie Dewart, Gregory Baum, and Avery Dulles to dehellenize, refocus, and revitalize the individual's experience of faith in the American Catholic situation in the 1970s represent one phase in the confrontation between theology and the secular. The diversity among these three, the personal quality of their newly chosen methodologies, and their alliance with the Catholic church and with a transcendent concept of God (as both of these are reconceived in their theologies) contribute to the form of their secular theologies as they are distinguished, for example, from the death-of-God movement only a few years before. The theologies of Dewart, Baum, and Dulles are self consciously contingent, relative, transient, and existential interpretations of a Catholic faith in dynamic evolutionary movement toward future recastings.

HANS KÜNG

Hans Küng is a leading Catholic theologian of our day, perhaps second only to Karl Rahner, the "Paul Tillich" of recent and contemporary Catholic theology. Even though Küng resides in Europe he is included here because of his extensive influence on American theology and his frequent visits to the United States. Küng is also one of the most controversial Catholic thinkers of our time, and, unlike the other three theologians we have discussed, has been in constant conflict with the Vatican. Basic to Küng's challenge is his concern that the church has failed to act on the reforms authorized by Vatican II. In making this challenge he has also questioned the structure of the church, the nature of the papacy, and the role of the priest.

When in 1959 Pope John XXIII called for an ecumenical council, Küng wrote a paper attacking the notion that the Catholic church is the sole depository of divine truth. He insisted that the Church is always in need of reform. Overnight Küng became a celebrity. The German bishops made him an advisor at Vatican II. That same year Küng published another book in which he calls into question the traditional Catholic view concerning the organization of the early church. He argues that nowhere does Jesus suggest the kind of church hierarchy that has dominated the church since the third century or the power given to the priests since that time. He contends that if a group of Christians wants to celebrate the eucharist and there is no ordained priest present, the Holy Spirit will provide the authenticity to make it a valid eucharist. The implication here is that the monarchical structure of the church—pope to bishop to priest to laymen—was not mandated by Jesus at all, nor even the origins of papal power nor the claim that the popes were the successors of the Apostles in a direct, unbroken line.

Pope Paul VI became pope in 1963 upon the death of John XXIII. Paul was no creative scholar in tune with modern thinking. His thinking was traditional, demanding the exposition of dogmas in their ancient creedal forms. This is in contrast to the thinking of contemporary Catholic theologians like Gregory Baum, Leslie Dewart, and Hans Küng who understand dogmas, not as conceptual propositions, but as historical formulations that can be better experienced than explained. Thus, the Pope and Küng were on a collision course.

In 1963 Küng was refused permission to lecture at the Catholic University in Washington, D.C. and Cardinal McIntyre of Los Angeles refused to let Küng appear in that diocese. However, he lectured on other campuses across the country and attacked the Catholic church for its "unfreedom" and "power politics." When Vatican II ended in 1965, Küng joined other young Catholic theologians in demanding immediate reform to implement the teachings of the Council. When such reform was not forthcoming, Küng became even more radical. In 1967 Küng published a book entitled *The Church* (the English version of which he dedicated to Michael Ramsey, the Archbishop of Canterbury) in which he stated, among other things, that the pope should above all consider himself as the servant of the Church and that this notion should be extended "to include the possibility of the pope having to resign," that "the Church never exists for the pope, the pope always exists for the Church."[26] A year earlier in his book *Freedom Today* he stated that "Every world religion is under God's grace and can be a way of salvation . . . and we may hope that everyone is."[27]

At about the same time Pope Paul declared a *vacatio legis,* a temporary voiding of the law, holding off the implementation of many of the Council's decisions until the Curia could prepare an official interpretation of these decisions. Such a step was immediately attacked by Küng and others. Yet the Pope did take some significant steps toward reform. He abolished the Index of Forbidden Books, reorganized the Roman Curia, eliminated many of the trappings of papal aristocracy, and inaugurated the Roman Synod of Bishops to serve as an advisory policy-making body.

But on doctrinal and other matters the Pope held the line. As far as Küng was concerned, the Pope's attempts at reform represented window dressing and did not get at the deeper issues of church reform. So Küng felt that the time had come to question the doctrine of papal infallibility on historical grounds and to rethink Catholic teaching on the nature of truth. In 1971 he published his most controversial book to date, *Infallible? An Inquiry.* In this book he documents an extensive list of doctrinal and historical errors in church pronouncements and also points out numerous instances in which the church had changed her mind; for example, in 1274 the Second Council of Lyons declared that non-Catholics were all going to hell, yet Vatican II said that there was salvation outside the church. In 1864 Pope Pius IX condemned liberalism and democracy; Vatican II affirmed both beliefs. And so on. He also attacks the traditional interpretation of papal infallibility first promulgated in 1870 at Vatican I, an interpretation based, he insists, on outmoded forms of thought and a naive view of the universe. Here are two passages from his book.

> It can no longer be ignored that, contrary to the best intentions of the Pope and his advisors, the longer the teaching office is exercised by Pope and Curia, the more is it exercised in a way which—as previously in Church history, and from Rome—inflicts the worst damage on the unity and credibility of the Catholic Church.

> To err is human. To err is also ecclesiastical, to err . . . is papal: simply because Church and pope are also human and remain human.[28]

In place of infallibility Küng suggested that we think of the *indefectibility* of the Church, that is, the Church herself will persist in the truth in spite of all possible mistakes. The Church will persevere despite the odds and errors!

A year later he published another book entitled *Why Priests? For A New Church Ministry* which contains the following passages.

> From a New Testament point of view . . . the term "priest" should be dropped as a specific and exclusive term to identify people who have ministries in the Church, since, according to the New Testament view, all believers are "priests."

> One cannot maintain historically that the bishops are in a direct and exclusive sense the successors of the apostle and even less that they are the successors of the college of the Twelve.

> The number of seven sacraments is a product of history. It was unknown during the entire first millennium and appeared first in the twelfth century, without any claim to exclusivity.

> The Church's ministry of leadership does not have to be celibate; the single life need not be part of it. Even those in the Catholic Church who still defend celibacy . . . will admit that it is a matter of purely ecclesiastical law from the Middle Ages.

> The Church's ministry of leadership does not have to be exclusively male; it need not be a men's association. This means . . . the admission of women to all the Church's special ministries and to ordination.

> It should not be said that ordination was "instituted by Christ." There is not the slightest evidence for this.[29]

Now Küng came under attack from the Roman Curia. Vatican authorities summoned Küng to come to Rome several times to defend himself against charges of heresy. Küng refused on the grounds that the Vatican procedures would not be impartial. The Congregation for the Doctrine of the Faith published a document reaffirming traditional church teachings including papal infallibility, and in 1975 the Congregation told Küng directly that his teachings on infallibility and the Eucharist were wrong and that he should stop professing them. Küng, of course, refused to acquiesce. When the Cardinal of Munich, Germany, was asked whether he was going to try to enforce the Vatican's strictures against Küng, Cardinal Döpfner replied that such a step would be foolish, explaining, "His books are already best-sellers without our assistance." In former days Küng probably would have been suspended from his priestly functions and had his books placed on the Index of Forbidden Books, and, finally, he would have been excommunicated. But the pressures of the modern world, the spirit of Vatican II, and increasing diversity of thought within the Catholic church have made it very difficult for anyone these days to be considered a full-fledged heretic. Küng himself apparently has no intention of leaving the church. He does not consider himself to be on the far edge of the church, but, rather, at the very center of the church of the future. His book *On Being a Christian* (1976) is probably the outstanding major theological treatise of the decade. In this book he denies the historicity of the resurrection and the virgin birth and declares that the reason why one should be a Christian these days is "in order to be truly human."[30]

By 1979, however, Hans Küng had gone too far for John Paul II. The Pope removed Küng's canonical mission to teach on the Catholic faculty at Tübingen. Although the Pope's action provoked a furious controversy, Küng remains *persona non grata*. He continues as director of the Ecumenical Institute and as professor of ecumenical theology at Tübingen, but Catholic students can no longer take courses for credit from him.

By the end of the 1970s Catholic theologians were grappling furiously with the age-old problem of how theology should accommodate itself to the secular world. How does the believer of today affirm faith in God and Christ within the larger context of a world in which the necessity of such a God and Christ is no longer as apparent as it once was? The theologians we have mentioned in this chapter have continued their reappraisal of Catholic doctrine and practice, often impatient with the progress of the church and often in disagreement with one another. Leslie Dewart has become disenchanted with the church, recently asserting:

> Since the end of Vatican II, the Catholic church has become, in my opinion, the single most effective hindrance to the evolution of man's religious consciousness. Yet, but for human folly, ignorance and fear, its role might well have become the diametrically opposite one. Man will most likely survive this tragic setback and prosper—even religiously—nonetheless. But to have had to live through this incredible, colossal historical failure is a profound disappointment to those of us who once glimpsed the possibility of a new religious age opening up for mankind in our time.[31]

Gregory Baum has left the priesthood and has become more interested in the sociology of knowledge as evidenced by his book *Religion and Alienation* (1975). *The Ecumenist,* edited by Baum, is a lively forum for Roman Catholic liberal theology. Many theologians other than the ones we have mentioned in this chapter have entered the fray. Of particular significance are Rosemary Ruether (discussed in the chapter on feminist theology) and David Tracy. Tracy's book *Blessed Rage for Order: The New Pluralism in Theology* (1975) argues for a revisionist model for theology to grapple with the dilemmas of the modern believer. For Tracy the modern Christian theologian

> finds himself disenchanted with the mystifications promulgated by too many church officials and the mystifications proclaimed with equal certitude by the secularist self-understanding of the age. He believes he shares the basic Christian faith of the former and the secular faith of the latter. Indeed, he believes that the Christian faith is at heart none other than the most adequate articulation of the basic faith of secularity itself. He also realizes that his understanding of Christianity must take a revisionist form which takes proper account of the cognitive, ethical and existential crises of much traditional Christian self-understanding. No longer can his secular faith find adequate articulation through the model for rational reflection developed by the Age of Enlightenment. Rather, this model must yield to one which can account for those insights developed since the "liberal" period and simultaneously negate those illusions of liberal secularity which both recent history and recent reflection have brought to light.[32]

In his book *The Resilient Church* (1977) Avery Dulles attacks David Tracy's "revisionist" stance, calling it "latent heresy" in its treatment of the Christian story as the "supreme fiction." He also finds Tracy guilty of capitulating to secularity:

> Nowhere does Tracy suggest that Christian revelation might challenge or correct the basic secular faith or transvalue its implicit values. Wherever a conflict appears between Christian commitment and the faith of secularity, it is the former rather than the latter which must be revised.[33]

Bernard Lonergan, a Catholic philosopher-theologian in the classical tradition, has received world-wide recognition for his scholarly efforts to develop a systematic theology that reflects the contemporary situation while remaining solidly grounded in neo-Thomistic thought. Lonergan recognizes that theology can no longer be the deductive discipline based on assumptions from scripture and tradition that it was in the scholastic period. Theology must now be an inductive science which utilizes data from both the past and the present. He writes:

> To follow Aquinas today is not to repeat Aquinas today, but to do for the twentieth century what Aquinas did for the thirteenth. As Aquinas baptized key elements in Greek and Arabic culture, so the contemporary Catholic philosopher and/or theologian has to effect a baptism of key elements in modern culture.[34]

Recent books by this intellectual heavyweight include *Insight: A Study of Human Understanding* (1970), *The Way To Nicea* (1976), and *Method in Theology* (1979).

The theological recastings proposed by the theologians discussed in this chapter and others like them contribute to a composite picture of theology at the end of the 1970s which is pluralistic, flexible, and evolving, grounded in human experience and oriented toward humanity-at-large in the secular realm. This same portrait can be seen in recent approaches toward ethical problems. For example, the Catholic Theological Society in a recent study of sexual ethics concludes that sexual behavior should be judged by whether it is conducive to "creative growth of the human person" and whether it affirms such values as self-liberation, other-enrichment, honesty, faithfulness, social responsibility, life-service and joy. Further, "Sexual intimacy may be an appropriate expression of the quality and depth of a relationship, whether marriage is intended or not."[35] Thus, "situation ethics" has become as much a part of left-wing Catholic thinking as has situational theology.

The advice Karl Rahner gave to the German Church in *The Shape of The Church to Come* (1974) is well worth remembering as we enter the 1980s: that the Church "should consider the fluidity and indefiniteness of her frontiers in a *positive* way."[36] This positive attitude toward fluid, pluralistic, indefinite, evolving, borders of Catholic belief once considered so threatening to the Church may be the cornerstone of future Catholic theologies. However, if mainstream Catholic theology follows the Protestant neo-evangelical trend and veers in the direction of a recovered emphasis on the supernatural, this will involve a reevaluation of the secular theological stance. Nevertheless, thanks to the left flank in Catholic theology, the Church has acquired an undeniable human or secular dimension. In 1977 Notre Dame University hosted a colloquium with the theme: "Toward Vatican III: The Work That Needs to Be Done." In attendance were seventy-one theologians and social scientists who together discussed the major theological issues facing the Catholic church in the future. Hans Küng urged a closing of the ranks between Catholic and Protestant theologians.

> The doctrinal discussions with the Reformation churches must be pursued with all possible commitment in order that significant agreements can be reached in the near future and so proclaimed as officially binding.

And David Tracy pleaded for the recognition of a genuine pluralism in meeting the challenges of our day.[37]

Some Catholic theologians are wondering whether in this time of pluralism it is possible to reach a consensus in Catholic theology. Leonard Swidler's edited work *Consensus in Theology?* (1980) provides a forum for eighteen theologians to respond to essays by Hans Küng and Edward Schillebeeckx, another theologian whose views have been challenged by the Vatican. Rosemary Ruether believes that consensus is not possible.

> For the foreseeable future we cannot expect a new consensus in the Catholic Church. This itself perhaps represents an artificial and static ideal. Rather we must seek to defend the survival of both of these critical options, conciliar and liberation theologies. We can do this only by limiting the power and authority of the Vatican and the hierarchy. This means not just theological but ecclesiastical pluralism in the Church—in effect, an internal schism. This pluralism does not exist as a tolerated right of free thought, but rather as a standoff in the struggle against an institution which does not concede the right of any other view to exist outside its own authority.[38]

Perhaps Dickens' phrase "the best of times, the worst of times" provides the best description of the 1970s in Catholic theology. The future direction of Catholic theology will be determined in large part by the new Pope John Paul II—whether he will follow the liberal innovative Pope John XXIII or the conservative tradition-bound Pope Paul VI. Although in his visit to the United States in the fall of 1979 he sounded like a conservative on doctrinal and church matters—and subsequent statements and actions have followed the conservative line—his new and growing exposure to theological pluralism may eventually lead him to a new understanding of faith and practice. Richard P. McBrien, in a recent article entitled "The Roman Catholic Church: Can It Transcend The Crisis?," writes:

> Pope John Paul II has the power to free that creative energy if he chooses. It is still too early to tell which ecclesiological and pastoral instincts will eventually dominate his pontificate: his theological commitment to collegiality or his culturally conditioned concerns about nuns' habits and priestly celibacy. Which of two predecessors will guide his ministry—John XXIII or Paul VI? If John, the renewal of the Catholic Church will be advanced; if Paul, the tensions and conflicts of the past 15 years will intensify, and Catholicism will have to wait at least another generation (and another papacy) to emerge from its present trauma.[39]

8

The Future of American Theology

This book has surveyed the major trends in American Christian theology during the past two decades. The contention has been that the primary weakness in the theologies of the 1970s has been their tendency to overemphasize one particular area or issue to the neglect of other equally important dimensions of life. To use the phrases employed in the Preface, the "inner history" of these theological perspectives has been stressed at the expense of their "outer history." A second major weakness has been their concentration on the activity of God with a lack of concern for the problem of God's existence and nature. The future of American theology lies in the development of a theological stance that encompasses and even transcends the boundaries of race, class, sex, and even historical religion, a theology centered in a view of the nature of God in harmony with the modern believer's reason and experience.

THE UNIVERSAL DIMENSION OF RELIGION

Religious and cultural pluralism will be the major challenge for American theologians in the 1980s. A recognition of one human family undergirding this pluralism represents the most pressing need. The major living religions of the world have a splendid opportunity to help realize this human interdependence. Insofar as they cooperate in this common mission, they will play an expanding role in the modern world. Insofar as they fail to make the relationships linking different groups in society paramount, they will become increasingly irrelevant to the needs of the modern believer.

The breakdown of external authority, the rise of independent thinking, and the growth of religious pluralism should undercut narrowness of vision among modern Christian believers. It should promote the search for that religion which, in terms of its breadth of outlook and meaningful symbols, can best help the individual solve the complex problems of a world of many different value systems. The goal is not that there should be one world religion any more than that there should be one big church, or that the particular elements of each religion—its historical traditions, its ceremonies, its dogmas—should be eliminated. One cannot be religious in a vacuum. Religions, like flowers, need roots and branches and leaves of various shapes and sizes; but the particular elements of all religions, like the flowers, are nourished by the same life-giving and life-sustaining Spirit. As long as human beings are different in terms of their backgrounds and use of symbols, religions must be rich in variety. One of the most significant features of Western and Eastern religions is not only their likeness in ethical concerns, but their differences of focus. Western religion has stressed social progress toward the kingdom, while Eastern religion has emphasized personal growth toward the enlightenment of the individual's soul. The modern believer is going to need both dimensions, somehow harmonized. Howard Thurman in *Footprints of a Dream,* the story of the founding of the Church for the Fellowship of All Peoples in San Francisco, has stated convictions which suggest the future of American theology.

> The journey from Rochester Theological Seminary to the Church for the Fellowship of All Peoples in San Francisco and later to Marsh Chapel, Boston University, carried me through many experiences, but always the purpose was the same. Religious experience must unite rather than divide men. There must be made available experiences by which the sense of separateness will be transcended and unity expressed, experiences that are deeper than all diversity but at the same time enriched by diversity.[1]

Perhaps it will be the test of time that will best lead us to this larger vision, for time has a way of minimizing human-made distinctions. The passage of years leads to the gradual lessening in importance of the historical factors that have divided humankind and the emergence of those moral principles common to all human beings.

THE TASK FOR THEOLOGIANS

Theologians should play a major role in articulating the universal dimension of religious experience. Unfortunately, the splinter theologies of the 1970s have failed the test, using a specific aspect of human experience as normative and thereby further dividing human beings into separate camps. Although these theologies have made indispensable contributions to the needs and aspirations of their own special interest groups, they have usually failed to grasp and articulate the wider implications of the theological task. Many black theologians have insisted that black experience is unique and, therefore, black theology must be different from "white" theology, "red" theology and so on. James Cone's attempt to link black theology with black power made it appear, as Major Jones suggests, that God was only on the side of the black person. But, of course, blacks have as much diversity in their particular experience as do whites, a fact which Cone confronted at the Conference of Third World Theologians in Ghana in 1977 when he was told he could never understand African black experience. He realized that common concerns require a dialogue with one another. The future of black theology lies with the thinking of theologians like Allen Boesak, who insists that racism is but one factor against which the struggle to overcome oppression should be waged. Malcolm X discovered this universal dimension late in his life on a pilgrimage to Mecca where he observed thousands of pilgrims of all races worshipping together. This experience changed his narrow racial perspective of the Nation of Islam to a more inclusive vision encompassing all oppressed peoples regardless of religion, race, or nationality.

Feminist theologians face the same challenge. Feminist experience cannot be the ultimate norm for theology nor can the cause of women be the only worthwhile issue. The oppression of women must be linked with all other forms of oppression in a common effort to eradicate inhumanity and injustice. Moreover, theology must also seek to liberate the oppressor as well as the oppressed. Rosemary Ruether reminds feminist theologians of this often-neglected goal:

> Any women's movement which is *only* concerned about sexism and no other form of oppression, must remain a women's movement of the white upper class, for it is *only* this group of women whose *only* problem is the problem of being women, since, in every other way, they belong to the ruling class. But a woman who belongs to other minority groups must inevitably refuse this monolithic analysis. She must integrate her struggle as a woman into the struggle to liberate her racial and socioeconomic group. Thus it seems to me essential that the women's movement reach out and include in its struggle the interstructuring of sexism with all other kinds of oppression, and recognize a pluralism of women's movements in the context of different groupings.

> Otherwise it will tend to remain a women's movement of the ruling class that can be misused to consolidate the power of that ruling class against the poor and nonwhite of both sexes.[2]

For South American liberation theologians the "South American experience"—even if there is such a thing—cannot be the final arbiter for theology. The time is past when they can refuse to dialogue with European and North American theologians and caricature European and North American theology as academic, dualistic, and unwittingly on the side of the oppressor. These theologians must be prepared both to teach and to learn as they confront other kinds of human oppression. Robert McAfee Brown underscores this point that liberation includes not only economic but also racial and sexual dimensions.

> The need is for widened theological dialogue, for there is conflict between various expressions of liberating theology. Black theologians, for example, tend to feel that Latin Americans stress economic oppression so much that they virtually ignore the racial component of oppression; to blacks, racism is as prevalent in socialist as in capitalist countries. Latin Americans respond that racial mentalities are enhanced by economic insecurity; this nourishes other insecurities and leads people to look for scapegoats who "deviate" from the norm. The conference on black theology, held in August 1977 in Atlanta, made clear that economic analysis was beginning to be taken more seriously by black theologians—an indication that the dialogue has proved fruitful. Similarly, North American feminist theologians charge (correctly) that South American liberation theologians have paid scant attention to the liberation of women; there have been subsequent contacts between the two groups so that the theme is beginning to appear on Third World agendas.[3]

Fortunately these splinter theologies are beginning to acknowledge a deeper understanding of the human condition that goes beyond race, sex, and economic status.

Similarly, evangelical theology is beginning to show broader comprehension of truth in different sources of human experience. Some evangelical theologians have broken out of the "we have the truth and you don't" circle to seek dialogue with alternative views. In this development Richard Quebedeaux is an effective spokesman.

> Evangelicals must recognize that no matter how convinced they are that they have "the truth" biblically, no one is promised *all* of that truth in this life. We see through a glass, darkly. Others—even Catholic and Protestant liberals—may have much to teach the evangelicals. Furthermore, God is the

ultimate judge of all our theologies, and Jesus has commanded us to love everyone, whether liberal, evangelical, or atheist, even our enemies. This should itself provide sufficient grounds for dialogue, fellowship, and joint action among Christians of differing views.[4]

Catholic secular theology of the 1970s has been a promising development in seeking wider areas of agreement and dialogue. Hans Küng, Richard Penaskovic, and Raimundo Panikkar represent this prominent trend. Hans Küng insists, as we have noted, that the differences today between Catholics and Protestants are not doctrinal but, rather, post-Reformation attitudes which can now be overcome. Penaskovic argues that Roman Catholicism should adopt the Augsburg Confession, the Lutheran confession of faith adopted in 1530. He goes on to say:

> As a Catholic theologian I would say that today there are no theological opinions that with certainty can be pointed to as absolutely binding on Catholics or Lutherans of such a nature as to require and legitimate the separation of the two churches.[5]

Raimundo Panikkar has been unusually creative in promoting a positive relationship between Christianity and the religions of the East, particularly Hinduism and Buddhism. Born in Spain, the child of a Catholic mother and a Hindu father, he was nourished in both the Bible and the Vedas. Ordained a Catholic priest, he spent many years in India studying Indian religion and continues to divide his time between India and his teaching post at the University of California at Santa Barbara. He roots his Catholic faith in religious experience and maintains that the religions of East and West are like the different colors of the spectrum, each reflecting its particular vision of reality. He has summarized his own spiritual pilgrimmage as follows: "I "left" as a Christian, I "found" myself a Hindu and I "return" a Buddhist, without ever having ceased to be a Christian.'"[6] The task for American theologians is to enter into dialogue with one another, to break down human-made divisions of oppressor and oppressed, black and white, men and women, South American and European, North American and African, Catholic and Protestant, Christian and non-Christian, which have falsely separated human beings from one another and to seek that larger dimension of human experience which unites us all in dignity, justice, and equality.

NATURAL THEOLOGY

Another responsibility for American theologians is to enter the arena of debate about the larger issues affecting human destiny. One of the chief faults of neo-orthodoxy was its proclamation of a revealed theology at the expense of reason or natural theology. With this approach many theologians considered rational inquiry as inimical to divine revelation. They established their own truth claims and abdicated responsibility for defending their convictions in the arena of intellectual debate. This failure to present the gospel in an intelligent and meaningful fashion led to what the New Testament scholar Rudolf Bultmann called, "the bankruptcy of contemporary theology." He wrote that neo-orthodoxy

> . . . witnessed a movement away from criticism and a return to a naive acceptance of the kerygma. The danger both for theological scholarship and for the Church is that this uncritical resuscitation of the New Testament mythology may make the Gospel unintelligible to the modern world.[7]

The battle for the minds and hearts of most individuals will not be won by retreating behind an historical revelation-claim and denying the legitimacy of reason. The struggle must be fought through rigorous competition in the marketplace of ideas.

Similarly in the black and South American liberation theologies of the 1970s one finds little interest in developing a rational view of the nature of human life, nature, and God. The focus is so overwhelmingly on one social issue that so-called metaphysical questions are dismissed as irrelevant or "academic." Action takes precedence over reflection. Surely one can understand the contention of someone like South American liberation theologian Gustavo Gutiérrez that the main challenge to the Christian faith today comes not from the nonbeliever but from the nonhuman. The oppressed are obviously concerned above all with the basic necessities of life that every human being must have in order to survive with any sense of dignity. This same emphasis on the nonhuman at the expense of the nonbeliever has also undergirded most of black theology.

But to neglect the importance of right belief is to open the door wide to the lunatic fringe of religion so much in evidence in contemporary cults. Right belief is not the luxury of a privileged minority but a necessity for everyone in order to avoid superstition. Intellectual inquiry may not lead directly to religious faith, but it should make that faith a more likely alternative. Otherwise, anyone can believe anything. It is through "natural theology" based on human experience and reason that the believer can and should provide a proper framework for Christian convictions. The task is to clear away philosophical difficulties by honest and rigorous thinking. Peter Berger develops this thesis in his latest book, *The Heretical Imperative*.[8] He notes, as we have, that pluralism presents the biggest challenge to contemporary theology, because it calls into question the authority of each exclusive religious tradition. Berger maintains that those who wish to hold on to their religious tradition have three options. They can steadfastly reaffirm the authority of the past (deduction); they can secularize their tradition (reduction); or they can reinterpret their tradition for today (induction). Berger opts for the third alternative, insisting, as we have, both that Christian theology must be in harmony with experience and reason and also that there should be a rapprochement between the religions of East and West.

Three issues in particular need to be explored thoroughly if the Christian alternative is to remain a live option for today. First, there is the problem of what is authentic knowledge and reliable sources for such knowledge. Second, what makes a person human and thereby capable of different kinds of knowledge? Third, the basic theological issue is who or what is the most real, that is, God? All three of these problems are interrelated. How one solves any one of them has important implications for solving the other two.

THE PROBLEM OF KNOWLEDGE

How do we know that we know? What are valid ways of obtaining information? William McLoughlin maintains that the roots of today's religious awakening lie in a basic revision of epistemology and ontology now underway. He finds people reframing the traditional questions: how do we know what is basic and how do we relate to what is real? Some individuals begin with the hypothesis that the only sure road to knowledge is by means of the scientific method. If the proponents of this "method" are suggesting that one should be careful and thorough and patient in one's investigations, their efforts should be applauded. However, if their hidden assumption is that only publicly verifiable knowledge is acceptable, then they have entered the arena of philosophical debate. The most rigid and uncompromising kind of modern fundamentalism takes the form of scientism which insists that only laboratory-centered research can give us authentic information about the nature of the individual and the larger world. These modern fundamentalists need to be reminded that securing genuine data on the various aspects of human experience requires a willingness to meet the conditions for achieving such knowledge in those areas.

Just as there are criteria of public verifiability and reduplication that the scientist must fulfill in laboratory experiments, so too, are there requirements to be achieved in such disciplines as music, art, and religion. The attainment of such knowledge is no less rigorous than laboratory techniques—perhaps more so—and the conditions are of equal importance. The seeker for religious knowledge, for example, must be willing to spend a considerable amount of time and energy in disciplined study and the "laboratory experience" of prayer and worship. The knowledge of God, like the knowledge of our inner selves, is analogous to knowing the beauty of a picture. This kind of knowledge is not susceptible to publicly verifiable criteria. Rather, it is the kind of knowledge that is achieved and authenticated through personal encounter. The failure to verify repeatedly and publicly such knowledge does not thereby make it less real; rather, it only makes it more difficult to communicate. For this reason the true mystic remains silent, knowing that a religious experience cannot be satisfactorily communicated to someone else. To deny the possibility of knowledge of God is sheer prejudice. The philosopher George Santayana once said that whoever searched the heavens with a telescope would no sooner find God than would one seeking the human mind by searching the human brain with a microscope. What one discovers in life is largely dependent on how one is looking. The problem of knowledge is exceedingly complex and difficult, but the point to be underscored is that religious knowledge can become significant only if the expectations are faithfully met. These expectations include an openness to those kinds of experiences that seem to come only through personal involvement, sensitivity, and prayer. Our knowledge of other people comes not so much through our own initiative, but by our willingness to let others reveal themselves to us. And so it is with our awareness of deeper levels of experience. Elton Trueblood puts the matter succinctly when he writes, "Truth is revealed in religion not just to anybody, but only to those who seek, and to those who care."[9] The theologian must continually press this point.

THE PROBLEM OF HUMAN NATURE

What or who is the human being? Is the person just a bit of protoplasm gone astray or a complicated computer of programmed material? Is humankind a little higher than the apes or a little less than the angels? This is another crucial philosophical problem which has important consequences. If the human being is just a complex machine, then there is no such thing as genuine freedom, values, or even "scientific truth." Either one is free—to a degree—or one is a prisoner of a chain of causes. Either one genuinely pursues goals or one's freedom is pure illusion. Kierkegaard once said that although one understands life backwards, one lives life forwards. Why should we assume that the backward look, which makes it appear as though one's life were completely determined, is a more reliable view of our complete nature than the forward look which makes freedom appear genuine? Any adequate theory of human nature must take into account the emergence of the unexpected and the role of the indeterminate.

Further, there is the problem of human status on the ladder of evolution. Compared to lower forms of life, humankind is not merely a higher animal but a new kind of animal, self-conscious and self-aware. William Pollard speculates:

> In spite of this evident continuity with everything else about him, there remains in man much which has no parallel with anything else in nature. His imagination and thoughts; his self-awareness and freedom; his memories, anticipations, and anxieties; his aspirations which by persistence of will accomplish so many remarkable things, and above all today, his knowledge of mathematics, science, and technology. How is he to understand that he is part of nature, and yet possesses such attributes which he finds nowhere else in nature? . . . Does this not point to a uniqueness which he perhaps never suspected in himself before? . . . In my own approach to the problem I have not found any better way . . . to understand its significance than to say that with the appearance of *Homo sapiens* thirty-five thousand years ago there had at last been produced a creature who alone, among all the manifold species of life, was made in the image of his creator.[10]

THE PROBLEM OF GOD

What is the nature of ultimate reality, that is, God? A major role for theology is to ask these larger questions. Harvey Cox is on target when he writes:

> Despite the efforts of some modern theologians to sidestep it, whether God exists or not is a desperately serious issue. All the palaver about the terms *existence* and *being* and all the sophisticated in-group bickering about nonobjectifying language cannot obscure the fact that there remains an indissoluble question after all the conceptualizations have been clarified. . . . Is man alone in the universe or not?[11]

Eminent Roman Catholic theologian Karl Rahner puts the matter very succinctly: "Is human existence absurd or does it possess comprehensive, ultimate meaning? The theologian, the person with faith, says there is ultimate significance."[12] To refuse to explore this ontological question intelligently is to become party to all sorts of superstitious nonsense. Obviously one's perception of the nature of reality depends essentially on how one has solved the problem of knowledge; these issues are interdependent. If one insists that there is only one way of obtaining information—the way of cold, impersonal fact from the laboratory of the scientist—then ultimate reality will remain essentially cold, impersonal fact. If however, one assumes the possibility of different levels of knowledge through love and beauty, then ultimate reality may reveal various stages of being that are mental and spiritual in character. The late Archbishop William Temple underscored this conviction.

> That the world should give rise to minds which know the world involves a good deal concerning the nature of the world. . . . The more completely we include Mind within Nature, the more inexplicable must Nature become except by reference to Mind.[13]

Consider, for example, the most significant fact about human nature, namely, personality. If one accepts the remarkable appearance of personality in the process of evolution, the more incomprehensible must reality become without allowing for the presence of a Thou. For, just as the third act of a play usually contains the chief clue to the plot of the entire drama so, too, might the appearance of consciousness on the scene of history reveal the deepest character of life itself.

The problem of God is unavoidable. Each individual has a view of reality, explicit or implicit. No one can escape seeking answers to the ultimate issues of human life and destiny. To refuse to confront intelligently belief in God on the grounds that the challenge to Christian faith comes today from the nonhuman and not the nonbeliever is simply bad theology. The Christian faith affirms the humanity of every individual because every individual is a child of God. It is God who makes us who we are. How can one accept this claim unless one is convinced of its truth? Nor can one afford to hide in the shell of an authoritarian revelation claim. It may be comforting to say that the only conclusive evidence in favor of the existence of a personal God is supernatural revelation, whether that declaration is guaranteed by the infallible teaching voice of the church or by the biblical proclamation. But how, then, can one know which church or which biblical interpreter speaks for God? Our best hope is to struggle through the muddy waters of rational inquiry in seeking an acceptable view of life's basic character and ultimate reality.

There is a need today for a natural theology. Reasonable people do disagree on what is philosophically tenable, but this conflict is to be found as much in economics and politics as it is in theology. It is a mark of our finitude. The fact that there are differences of opinion does not mean that we should discard the priority and use of rational inquiry. Rather, it means that we should be more circumspect and patient and humble. The theology of the future should strive for a vision of God, humanity, and the world that is consistent with our best thinking and our deepest experiences.

THE REDISCOVERY OF THE SACRED

Scientific materialism, that is, a narrow scientism which stipulates that reality must be material, measurable, and publicly verifiable is clearly no longer a viable world view. What we are discovering is that the deeper we probe any one segment of reality, the more we begin to comprehend the interrelatedness of all knowledge and experience, to understand that there is a fundamental unity to existence. For this very reason, the biologists today are becoming chemists, the chemists, physicists; the physicists, astronomers, the astronomers, theologians; and the theologians, biologists.

This transformation of the human outlook has opened up new

dimensions of reality heretofore untapped. It betrays a movement in the direction of a rediscovery of the sacred or transcendent as essential to an understanding of the fullness of life. This deepening of the scope of human awareness in other fields suggests the future of theology. In the seventies several religious trends emerged suggesting a quest for truth that beckons from beyond the secular dimension: the renaissance of mysticism, the resurgence of Eastern religions, the findings of depth psychology, the popularity of faith healing, the bankruptcy of materialism, the renewed interest in psychical phonemena, and so on. These developments contain "signals of transcendence," to use Peter Berger's phrase, which point to other levels of experience beyond the secular here-and-now. To be sure, the "turning to the East" phenomenon carries with it a good deal of naivité and humbuggery, a point that Gita Mehta makes in her hilarious book *Karma Cola: Marketing the Mystic East* (1979).[14] Carl Raschke's *The Interruption of Eternity* (1980) indicates that this phenomenon represents a retreat from the real world.[15] Yet on the positive side this rediscovery of the sacred is a recognition of the richness and mystery of reality that had been suffocated by the secular world view. It points to a view of ultimate reality, mystical in character, that permeates and even unites humanity and nature with the cosmos. William McLoughlin makes much the same point in writing of a Fourth Great Awakening (1960–1990) which

> will most likely include a new sense of the mystical unity of all mankind and of the vital power of harmony between man and nature. The godhead will be defined in less dualistic terms, and its power will be understood less in terms of an absolutist, sin-hating, death-dealing "Almighty Father in Heaven" and more in terms of a life-supporting, nurturing, empathetic, easygoing parental (Motherly as well as Fatherly) image. The nourishing spirit of mother earth, not the wrath of any angry father above, will dominate religious thought.[16]

Feminist theologians have been particularly insightful in pointing toward a more holistic and communal world view. Rosemary Ruether has traced this pattern of a mystical unity of nature and humanity to the earliest times of recorded history, a pattern which remained dominant until the early Christian era when nature and humanity came to be considered alien to one another. Thus there emerged a dualism in Western thinking that has continued to this day. Ruether opts for a view of God as the empowering spirit who is the foundation of our unity and existence.[17] Carol Ochs urges a view of deity that discerns unity in all things, suggesting that God is not separate from other aspects of reality, that we are All in All.[18] And Sheila Collins argues for a multidimensional view of reality that makes it possible for us to accept variety and live with ambiguity in a spirit-filled world.[19] Indeed, it appears as though a redefinition of God is moving us closer to the traditional Hebraic world view.

The Hebrew word for spirit is *Ruach*, which signifies breath or wind. For this reason the ancient Hebrew refused to speak the name Yahweh, which was an early name for deity in that tradition. To utter this name would be to try to capture and thereby degrade this spirit. It is for this reason that theologians like Robinson, Schillebeeckx, and Dewart have suggested that either we remain silent about God or find new terminology; and Mary Daly notes the poverty of all our symbols of God, our need to rename the cosmos. God is like the breath or wind, the life-giving force which is real, but which must be symbolized by word images which suggest non-physical power: awe, wonder, mystery, creativity, sacredness, reverence. Keeping in mind that a description of God is well nigh impossible, what other terms can be used that will help, however inadequately, to spell out the fundamental affirmation that God is spirit?

God is the term that one uses to identify the fundamental unity of all existence and experience. God is that spirit which makes it possible for there to be a *uni*verse. To ask whether God exists is to ask whether a *uni*verse exists. This same point is made by Bishop Robinson: "God is, by definition, ultimate reality. And one cannot argue whether ultimate reality *exists*. One can only ask what ultimate reality is like."[20]

This concept of unity in existence is a necessary principle which both the advocate of science and the advocate of religion affirm. The scientist has the faith that there is a oneness in reality, that the same "laws" apply as much on the other side of the moon as they do on this earth. The scientist assumes that when an astronaut lands on the moon, one does not discover a whole new set of principles of motion and energy, but one may gather new information to refine the present concepts. There is continuity from atom to amoeba to astronaut. One's comprehension of reality may change, but the principle of unity remains. The philosopher Alfred North Whitehead stresses this point: ". . . there can be no living science unless there is a widespread instinctive conviction in the existence of an *Order of Things*, and, in particular, of an *Order of Nature*."[21] The religious person confesses this same conviction. The believer proclaims that the God in whom one lives and moves and has one's being is one God. "Hear, O Israel, the Lord our God is one."

God is also the spirit of meaning. God is that which makes life worth living. God is that which gives human existence ultimate meaning, as Karl Rahner puts it. God is present wherever life is affirmed as significant. In other words, God is the dimension of the *Sacred*. The two-storied universe has given us the distorted notion that some things are intrinsically sacred, while others are inherently secular. The church is sacred, the world is secular. "Religious relics" are sacred, the love of money as the root of all evil is secular. For a person to be religious in this sense has usually meant for the individual to withdraw into a special kind of "holy life," like that of the monk, considered to be the highest calling. It is a sacred vocation because it sets one off from the lower profane world. The implication here is that a supernatural Being has bestowed special prerogatives on select institutions, objects, and persons, endowing them with a sacred aura, while this same Being withholds such blessing from other institutions, objects, and persons, giving them a secular flavor. This dualism has often been the underlying rationale for sexism and racism, as Rosemary Ruether has pointed out. This dualism no longer holds. For the modern believer, sacred and secular are two different ways of looking at the same scene. The church can be secularized; the world can be made sacred. "Religious relics" can be secular; money can have a sacred use.

The late Martin Buber gave an eloquent portrayal of these differences of perspective in terms of his phrases I-It and I-Thou. He believed that one's relationship to the world and to other people is twofold, and in each of these relationships there is a different kind of knowledge which makes one's response different. In the I-It relationship one looks upon the other person or thing as an object to be manipulated for one's own ends. In the I-Thou relationship the other person or thing has its own identity and integrity. One cannot manipulate the other, for the moment that one does, the Thou becomes an It. The I-Thou perspective is the sacred. It enriches the other with meaning. The I-It perspective is the secular. It objectifies the other and strips it of self-meaning. God is the spirit of meaning or "the sacred dimension" that permeates life. God's presence is acknowledged when one affirms the Thouness of the other. Buber's point here is that in each Thou we are confronting the Eternal Thou. The common misconception is that sacred and secular apply to different things and persons. The truth is that persons and things take on their proper significance only insofar as they are enriched by meaning. God is the spirit of the sacred which hallows life. This spirit does not exist as a separate entity apart from humanity any more than the principle of ordered unity functions in a particular sphere. The error of the earlier tradition was to locate God divorced from humanity and the world. The principle of meaning can never be confined to one church or one religious tradition. God is present wherever there is found that creative thrust of spirit which can burst forth into every human life, that spirit which makes possible new insights and discoveries, which casts out fear and restores wholeness of life.

God is also the principle of hope. Where hope is present, God is present. Where hope is absent, God's presence is no longer acknowledged. Paul Tillich notes the difficulty in finding appropriate words and symbols that denote ultimate reality. He concludes:

> Perhaps you should call this depth hope, simply hope. For if you find hope in the ground of history, you are united with the great prophets who were able to look into the depth of their times, who tried to escape it, because they could not stand the horror of their visions, and who yet had the strength to look to an even deeper level and there to discover hope.[22]

The religious person is the person of hope who sees creative possibilities in every situation and who, therefore, refuses to give up the struggle for meaning. The modern believer affirms that good can emerge victorious over evil, that right can conquer wrong, that faith can transcend doubt. The believer acknowledges the reality of darkness, but insists that further light can always shine forth and illuminate life and the life of all humankind.

The religious person further asserts that meaning and hope find their highest fulfillment in and through love. To confess that God is the spirit of love is to say that God's presence is acknowledged wherever and whenever love is present. Love is the deep and abiding relationship of concern and trust that a person can have for another person or thing as subject. Love is basically sacrificial, for the person willingly gives of oneself for the sake of the other. Love is I-Thou. There is a deep hunger and need today for the acknowledgement of every human being as personal and having dignity in his or her own right. Each individual has inner worth. Each wants to be respected and trusted. Every individual knows that the only kind of life that will ever make sense is one in which this sacrificial redemptive relationship is supreme. Why is this? Because one lives in the kind of world that creates and sustains this love, that makes this value universal and supreme for each person, that is I-Thou in its deepest stirrings.

By way of summary, God is this basic ordered unity which is spirit by nature and which can best be poetically described by the dimensions of sacredness, meaning, hope, and love. This definition by no means exhausts the divine reality, and there may be other terms more appropriate to express the reality of these aspects. Although the philosopher William James wrote eighty years ago, his thoughts on the subject still speak to our needs today.

> The practiced needs and experiences of religion seem to me sufficiently met by the belief that beyond each man and in a fashion continuous with him there exists a larger power which is friendly to him and his ideals. All that the facts require is that the power should be both other and larger than our conscious selves. Anything larger will do, if only it be large enough to trust for the next step.[23]

THE ROLE OF JESUS

In Christian theology of the future the role of Jesus will underscore those universal qualities which he shares with the prophets of all traditions. The basic assumption will be that Jesus was first and foremost a human being. If the early Christians had been loyal to their Jewish heritage, instead of accommodating their teachings to a dualistic hellenistic framework, the priority of Jesus' full humanity would be more easily acknowledged.

Jesus should be placed by Christians squarely in the mainstream of the Jewish prophetic tradition. If Christians are willing to join with the Jews by incorporating their festivals, honoring their Holy Days, appreciating their lack of dogma, and studying their post-biblical history, then the portrayal of the fully Jewish Jesus that will emerge can be enlightening for both Christian and Jew. This would mean for both churches and synagogues a new era of cooperation in which the festivals of Christianity and Judaism, and even Hinduism and Buddhism, would be jointly celebrated. Krister Stendahl has indicated the need for a new understanding between Jews and Christians.

> Christian theology needs a new departure. And it is equally clear that we cannot find it on our own, but only by the help of our Jewish colleagues . . . We need to ask, in spite of it all, whether they are willing to let us become again part of their family, a peculiar part to be sure, but, even so, relatives who believe themselves to be a peculiar kind of Jew. Something went wrong in the beginning. I say "went wrong" for I am not convinced that what happened in the severing of the relations between Judaism and Christianity was the good and positive will of God. Is it not possible for us to recognize that we parted ways not according to but against the will of God?[24]

Certain contemporary trends suggest that the significance of Jesus for the future will depend to a large degree on whether his way of living—"the man for others"— can speak to the human condition in ways that fill one's life with meaning, hope, and love. On this point black theology and South American liberation theology have made a major contribution. These theologians have considered Jesus primarily as liberator, the one who frees human beings from all forms of oppression. Although James Cone is quite wrong in making close allies of Christianity and black power, he is quite right in describing Jesus as

> the man for others who views his existence as inextricably tied to other men to the degree that his own Person is inexplicable apart from others. The others, of course, refer to all men, especially the oppressed.[25]

In similar fashion Gustavo Gutiérrez asserts that Jesus as liberator "is at the heart of the historical current of humanity; the struggle for a just society is in its own right very much a part of salvation history."[26] This role of Jesus as liberator will be confirmed, not because the church or scripture give him stature, but because his quality of living—of sacrificial love, of "setting at liberty those who are oppressed"— fulfills humanity's deepest longing. The "Jesus model" is that of a life of complete service and sacrifice in love and truth to God and humanity, and in this respect he is "the way, the truth, and the life." He is the manifestation of sacredness, meaning, hope, and love. He is the incarnation of the I-Thou.

This concept of Jesus as the prophet of sacrificial love reflects the basic moral convictions of the major living religions of the world. The relationship that Jesus has to the Hebrew prophets is clear. There is also a kinship with the leading figures of other major religions. This ideal of sacrificial love reaches across the centuries to the great compassion of the Buddha who declared that hatred is not obliterated by hatred at any time but only by love. It bursts forth in the manifestation of soul-force emanating from Hinduism. It expresses itself in the power of non-violent resistance practiced so eloquently by Mahatma Gandhi, the Hindu whom the Christian Martin Luther King credited with enhancing his Christian witness. The ideal of sacrificial love unites rather than divides humankind. It makes the ultimate test of a believer one's life and not one's label. The "uniqueness" of Christ is to be found in his universality and the quality of his interpersonal relationships. This view of Christ as the incarnation of sacrificial love should be the cornerstone of a Christology for our day.

THE MISSION OF THE CHURCH

The impact of the scientific revolution has never been fully comprehended by the Christian church. In earlier days it opposed this revolution, fiercely resisting any world view or method of obtaining knowledge that seemed to interfere with its supernatural claims. One only needs to read Andrew White's monumental work, *History of the Warfare between Science and Theology* to find precise historical documentation of the continued intransigence of the church toward human progress. Indeed, a good case could be made for the thesis that the church has more often than not regarded progress in every area of human experience as heretical. The religious heresy of one age has usually become the orthodoxy of the next age, but only after bitter struggle.

What is the proper mission of the church of today? Its mission should be understood not by looking to the past for unity, but rather by boldly accepting the present and future moral imperative. The contributions made by the church today should be qualitative and not quantitative as it fosters a vision guided by its purpose and not retarded by its past, a mission determined solely by the dynamic impact that the sacrificial love manifested in Christ ought to make upon human lives. The high calling of the church is the deepening of the love of God and humanity. The theologies of the 1970s make their greatest contribution as they focus on the plight of the oppressed and the need for total human liberation.

What does the deepening of the love of God and humanity mean? In conclusion, here are a few examples of the proper mission for the future church. Racial and sexual discrimination should be abolished in every church as each individual life is brought under the discipline of sacrificial love. There must be a renewed dedication of the believer's time and talents to the cause of human justice and freedom, and a greater personal and corporate commitment to the welfare of those who suffer and are oppressed. Every human effort should be made to further greater understanding among the peoples of the world as Christians join with others of good will from all cultures and religions in a common effort to achieve the dignity of all humanity. This joining together does not mean the eventual emergence of one big church or religion or, to use Raimundo Panikkar's analogy, one single tower to the Lord. He writes:

> What would happen if we simply gave up wanting to build this tremendous unitarian tower? What if instead we were to remain in our small beautiful huts and houses and domes and start building roads of communication (instead of just transportation) which could in time be converted into ways of communion between and among the different tribes, lifestyles, religions, philosophies, colors, races, and all the rest? And even if we cannot quite give up the dream of a unitarian Mankind . . . could it not be met by just building roads of communication rather than some gigantic new empire, ways of communion instead of coercion, paths which might lead us to overstep our provincialisms without tossing us into a single sack, into a single cult, into the monotony of a single culture?[27]

The ideal of sacrificial love will be applied to the basic moral issues which face humankind today: war, racism, sexism, poverty, population explosion, international relations, ecology, technology, to mention a few. Believers will attempt to build a genuine world community based on hope and love. Underlying the mission of the church will be the spirit of sacredness which gives each person a sense of worth and dignity. The primary purpose of worship and prayer will be to foster this deeper spirit which produces a life filled with meaning, hope, and love—for this is humanity's highest destiny.

The Christian churches today stand perhaps on the edge of a meaningless future, one in which they will fight a losing battle for historic creeds while the real struggles of life and death are being waged outside their realm. Or, they could be on the growing edge of a new frontier of sacrificial love and dedicated discipleship, a frontier in which the deepening love of God and humanity becomes the very reason for their existence.

NOTES

CHAPTER 1

1 Morton Enslin, *The Protestant Credo,* ed. Vergilius Ferm (New York: Philosophical Library, 1953), p. 80.

2. Floyd Ross, Ibid., p. 90.

3. Walter Rauschenbusch, *A Theology for the Social Gospel* (New York: Abingdon Press, 1917), p. 48.

4. Harry Emerson Fosdick, *The Living of These Days* (New York: Harper, 1956), p. 230.

5. Harry Emerson Fosdick, *The Power to See It Through* (New York: Harper, 1935), p. 133.

6. Harry Emerson Fosdick, *The Living of These Days,* p. 66.

7. Ibid., p. 258.

8. Ibid., p. 232.

9. J. Gresham Machen, *The Virgin Birth of Christ* (New York: Harper, 1930), p. 397.

10. Quoted in J. S. Bixler, *A Faith That Fulfills* (New York: Harper, 1951), p. 31.

11. Karl Barth, *The Word of God and the Word of Man* (Chicago: Pilgrim Press, 1928), p. 43.

12. Karl Barth, *Revelation,* ed. J. Baillie (New York: The Macmillan Co., 1937), pp. 48, 53, 45.

13. Floyd Filson, *Jesus Christ the Risen Lord* (New York: Abingdon Press, 1956), pp. 25, 31.

14. Sören Kierkegaard, *The Sickness unto Death* (New York: Doubleday Anchor Books, 1954), p. 257.

CHAPTER 2

1. *Time*, 30 March 1978.

2. Sidney Ahlstrom, *A Religious History of The American People*, vol. 2. (New York: Doubleday, 1975), p. 600.

3. William McLoughlin, *Revivals, Awakenings, and Reform: An Essay on Religion and Social Change in America, 1607–1977* (Chicago: The University of Chicago Press, 1978), p. 1.

4. Paul Tillich, *The Protestant Era* (Chicago: The University of Chicago Press, 1963), p. 202.

5. Gordon Allport, *The Individual and His Religion* (New York: The Macmillan Co., 1954), pp. 35–36.

6. Sidney Ahlstrom, "The Radical Turn in Theology and Ethics: Why It Occurred in the 1960s," *Religion in American History: Interpretive Essays*, eds. John M. Mulder and John F. Wilson (Englewood Cliffs, New Jersey: Prentice-Hall, Inc., 1978), p. 448.

7. Hans Küng, *On Being a Christian* (New York: Doubleday, 1976), pp. 502–503.

8. McLoughlin, *Revivals, Awakenings, and Reform*, p. 191.

9. Dietrich Bonhoeffer, *Letters and Papers from Prison* (New York: The Macmillan Co., 1953; paperback edition, 1962), pp. 162, 163, 166, 222–223, 219.

10. John Robinson, *Honest To God* (Philadelphia: The Westminster Press, 1963), p. 49.

11. John Cobb and David Ray Griffin, eds., *Process Theology: An Introductory Exposition* (Philadelphia: The Westminster Press, 1976), p. 43.

12. Ibid., p. 53.

13. William Hamilton, *The New Essence of Christianity* (New York: Association Press, 1961), p. 58.

14. Thomas Ogletree, *The Death of God Controversy* (New York: Abingdon Press, 1966), p. 42.

15. William Hamilton, *On Taking God out of the Dictionary* (New York: McGraw-Hill, 1974), pp. 18–19.

16. Paul van Buren, *The Secular Meaning of the Gospel* (New York: The Macmillan Co., 1963), p. 103.

17. Ved Mehta, *The New Theologian* (New York: Harper & Row, 1965), p. 66.

18. Van Buren, *Secular Meaning*, p. 157.

19. Thomas Altizer, *The Gospel of Christian Atheism* (Philadelphia: The Westminster Press, 1966), pp. 54, 57.

20. Ibid., p. 15.

21. Richard Rubenstein, *After Auschwitz* (Indianapolis, Indiana: Bobbs-Merrill, Co., 1966), p. 152.

22. Ibid., p. 153.

23. Ibid., p. 225.

24. Harvey Cox, *The Secular City* (New York: The Macmillan Co., 1965), p. 255.

25. Jürgen Moltmann, *Theology of Hope* (New York: Harper & Row, 1967), p. 164.

26. Wolfhart Pannenberg, *The Idea of God and Human Freedom* (Philadelphia: The Westminster Press, 1973), p. 93.

27. Peter Berger, *A Rumor of Angels (New York: Doubleday, 1969), p. 23.*

28. Langdon Gilkey, *Naming the Whirlwind: The Renewal of God-Language* (New York: Bobbs-Merrill, 1969), p. 283.

29. Ibid., p. 469.

CHAPTER 3

1. Benjamin Mays, *The Negro's God as Reflected in His Literature* (Boston: Chapman & Grimes, 1938), p. 253.

2. Sergio Torres and Virginia Fabella, eds., *The Emergent Gospel* (Maryknoll, New York: Orbis Books, 1976), p. 79.

3. Benjamin Mays, *Born to Rebel* (New York: Scribners, 1971), p. 2.

4. Martin Luther King, *Why We Can't Wait* (New York: New American Library, 1964), p. 86.

5. William Grier and Price Cobbs, *Black Rage* (New York: Basic Books, 1968), p. 200.

6. Joseph Washington, *The Politics of God: The Future of the Black Churches* (Boston: Beacon Press, 1967), p. 162.

7. Ibid., p. 227. Note that Washington is still using the term *negro* instead of *black*.

8. Grier, *Black Rage*, p. 4.

9. Albert Cleage, *The Black Messiah* (New York: Sheed & Ward, 1968), p. 98.

10. Robert Lecky and Elliott Wright, *Black Manifesto: Religion, Racism and Reparations* (New York: Sheed & Ward, 1969), p. 119.

11. James Cone, *Black Theology and Black Power* (New York: The Seabury Press, 1969), p. 1.

12. Ibid., p. 6.

13. Ibid., p. 68.

14. Ibid., p. 117.

15. Ibid., p. 151.

16. James Cone, *A Black Theology of Liberation* (New York: J. B. Lippincott Co., 1970), p. 49.

17. Ibid., p. 118.

18. Ibid., p. 136.

19. Joseph Washington, *Black and White Power Subreption* (Boston: Beacon Press, 1969), p. 182.

20. Ibid., p. 206.

21. J. Deotis Roberts, *Liberation and Reconciliation: A Black Theology* (Philadelphia: The Westminster Press, 1971), pp. 20–21.

22. Ibid., p. 189.

23. Major Jones, *Black Awareness: A Theology of Hope* (Nashville: Abingdon Press, 1971), p. 115.

24. Ibid., p. 142.

25. J. Deotis Roberts and James A. Gardiner, eds., *Quest for a Black Theology* (Philadelphia: Pilgrim Press, 1971), p. 80.

26. Columbus Salley and Ronald Behm, *Your God Is Too White* (Downers Grove, Illinois: Intervarsity Press, 1971), p. 7.

27. Albert Cleage, *Black Christian Nationalism* (New York: William Morrow, 1972), p. 9.

28. Ibid., pp. 96, 174.

29. Ibid., p. 259.

30. Joseph Washington, *Black Sects and Cults* (New York: Doubleday, 1972), p. xi.

31. Gayraud Wilmore, *Black Religion and Black Radicalism* (New York: Doubleday, 1972), p. 304.

32. William Jones, *Is God a White Racist? A Preamble to Black Theology* (New York: Doubleday, 1973), p. 186.

33. James Cone, *God of the Oppressed* (New York: The Seabury Press, 1975), pp. 187–192.

34. Warner Traynham, *Christian Faith in Black and White* (Wakefield, Mass.: Parameter Press, 1973), p. 65.

35. Deotis Roberts, *A Black Political Theology* (Philadelphia: The Westminster Press, 1974), p. 222.

36. Ibid., p. 193.

37. Ibid., p. 16.

38. Ibid., pp. 122–123.

39. Major Jones, *Christian Ethics for Black Theology: The Politics of Liberation* (Nashville: Abingdon Press, 1974), p. 193.

40. Julius Lester, "Be Ye Therefore Perfect," *Katallagate*, Winter, 1974, pp. 25–26.

41. James Cone, *God of the Oppressed*, p. 17.

42. Ibid., p. 137.

43. Ibid., p. 245.

44. Cecil Cone, *The Identity Crisis in Black Theology* (Nashville: African Methodist Episcopal Church, 1975), p. 90.

45. Ibid., p. 122.

46. Ibid., p. 137.

47. Ibid., p. 141.

48. Ibid., pp. 143–144.

49. Warner Traynham, *Black Theology Lecture Series* (St. Petersburg, Florida, 1977), pp. 23–24.

50. James Cone, *Union Seminary Quarterly Review*, vol. 31, no. 1, Fall 1975, pp. 81–82.

51. James Cone, "Black Theology & The Black Church," *Cross Currents*, vol. 27, no. 2, (Summer 1977), pp. 147–156.

52. Henry Mitchell, *Black Belief: Folk Beliefs of Blacks in America* (New York: Harper & Row, 1975), p. 9.

53. Allan Boesak, "Coming in out of the Wilderness," *The Emergent Gospel: Theology from the Underside of History*, eds. Sergio Torres and Virginia Fabella (Maryknoll, New York: Orbis, 1976), p. 88.

54. Allan Boesak, *Farewell to Innocence: A Social-Ethical Study of Black Theology and Black Power* (Maryknoll, New York: Orbis Books, 1976), p. 13.

55. Martin Garate, *Theology in The Americas*, eds., Sergio Torres and John Eagleson (Maryknoll, New York: Orbis Books, 1976), p. 356.

56. Peter Paris, *Black Leaders in Conflict* (New York: Pilgrim Press, 1978), p. 231.

57. Ibid., p. 229.

58. Calvin E. Bruce and William R. Jones, eds., *Black Theology II: Essays on the Formation and Outreach of Contemporary Black Theology* (Lewisburg, Pennsylvania: Bucknell University Press, 1978), pp. 20–21.

59. Ibid., p. 194, p. 196.

60. Ibid., p. 241.

61. Kofi Appiah-Kubi and Sergio Torres, eds., *African Theology En Route* (Maryknoll, New York: Orbis Books, 1979), p. 11.

62. Ibid., p. 177.

63. Ibid., pp. 177–178.

64. Gayraud Wilmore and James Cone, eds., *Black Theology: A Documentary History, 1969–1979* (Maryknoll, New York: Orbis Books, 1979), p. 3.

CHAPTER 4

1. Enrique Dussel, *Ethics and the Theology of Liberation* (Maryknoll, New York: Orbis Books, 1978), p. 10.

2. Sergio Torres and Virginia Fabella, eds., *The Emergent Gospel* (Maryknoll, New York: Orbis Books, 1976), p. 180.

3. Louis M. Colonness, ed., *Conscientization for Liberation* (Washington: Division For Latin America, U. S. Catholic Conference, 1971), p. 223.

4. C. Peter Wagner, *Latin American Theology: Radical or Evangelical? The Struggle for the Faith in a Young Church* (Grand Rapids, Michigan: Eerdmans, 1970), p. 17.

5. Enrique Dussel, *History and The Theology of Liberation* (Maryknoll, New York: Orbis Books, 1976), p. 117.

6. Wagner, *Latin American Theology*, p. 61.

7. Ibid., p. 24.

8. Martin Marty and Dean Peerman, eds., *New Theology No. 6* (New York: The Macmillan Co., 1969), pp. 131–134.

9. *Crosscurrents*, vol. 28, p. 10.

10. Colonness, *Conscientization*, p. 278.

11. Rosino Gibellini, ed., *Frontiers of Theology in Latin America* (Maryknoll, New York: Orbis Books, 1979), p. x.

12. Rubem Alves, *A Theology of Human Hope* (New York: World Publishing Co., 1969), p. 67.

13. Gibellini, *Frontiers*, p. 301.

14. Gustavo Gutiérrez, *A Theology of Liberation* (Maryknoll, New York: Orbis Books, 1971), p. ix.

15. Ibid., p. 2.

16. Ibid., p. 307.

17. Ibid., p. 285.

18. Gibellini, *Frontiers*, p. 28.

19. Sergio Torres and John Eagleson, eds., *Theology in the Americas* (Maryknoll, New York: Orbis Books, 1976), p. 312.

20. Sergio Torres, ed., *The Emergent Gospel* (Maryknoll, New York: Orbis Books, 1976), p. 247.

21. Dussel, *Ethics*, p. 26.

22. Jóse Miguez Bonino, *Doing Theology in a Revolutionary Situation* (Philadelphia: Fortress Press, 1975), p. 81.

23. Juan Luis Segundo, *Liberation of Theology* (Maryknoll, New York: Orbis Books, 1976), p. 3

24. Ibid., p. 94.

25. Gibellini, *Frontiers*, p. 170.

26. Wagner, *Latin American Theology*, p. 61.

27. Ibid., p. 79.

28. Hans Küng, *On Being a Christian* (New York: Doubleday, 1976), p. 565.

29. Robert McAfee Brown, *Theology in a New Key* (Philadelphia: The Westminster Press, 1978), p. 11.

30. Ibid., p. 191.

31. *Christianity and Crisis*, 29 March 1976, p. 57.

32. Ibid., p. 59.

33. Ibid., p. 62.

34. *Christianity and Crisis*, 17 September 1973, p. 170.

35. Ibid., p. 176. For further reading on the relationship between Reinhold Niebuhr's moral theology and South American liberation theology see Dennis P. McCann, *Christian Realism and Liberation Theology* (Maryknoll, New York: Orbis Books, 1981).

36. Rosemary Ruether, ed., *Liberation Theology* (New York: Paulist Press, 1972), p. 13.

37. Ibid., p. 16.

38. Schubert M. Ogden, *Faith and Freedom. Toward A Theology of Liberation* (Nashville: Abingdon Press, 1979), pp. 33–37, p. 73. Another book which relates process theology to liberation theology is Delwin Brown, *To Set At Liberty. Christian Faith and Human Freedom.* (Maryknoll, New York: Orbis Books, 1981).

39. *Christianity and Crisis*, 18 September 1978, p. 210.

40. Ibid., pp. 211, 218.

41. *Christianity and Crisis*, 19 March 1979, p. 59.

42. Torres, *Theology in the Americas*, p. 293.

43. Torres, *The Emergent Gospel*, p. 271.

44. John Eagleson and Philip Scharper, eds., *Puebla and Beyond: Documentation and Commentary* (Maryknoll, New York: Orbis Books, 1979), p. 346.

45. Ibid., p. 121.

CHAPTER 5

1. Judith Hole and Ellen Levine, *Rebirth of Feminism* (New York: Quadrangle Books, 1971), p. 85.

2. Valerie Saiving, "The Human Situation: A Feminine View," *Womanspirit Rising*, eds., Carol Christ and Judith Plaskow (New York: Harper & Row, 1979), p. 38, p. 41.

3. Elizabeth Achtemeier, *The Feminine Crisis in Christian Faith* (Nashville: Abingdon Press, 1965), pp. 34, 147.

4. Doris and Howard Hunter, "Neither Male nor Female," *The Christian Century*, 28 April 1965, p. 530.

5. Hannah Bonsey Suthers, "Religion and the Feminine Mystique," *The Christian Century*, 21 July 1965, p. 914.

6. Elsie Thomas Culver, *Women in the World of Religion* (New York: Doubleday, 1967), p. 113.

7. Sarah Bentley Doely, ed., *Women's Liberation and the Church* (New York: Association Press, 1970), p. 97, p. 102.

8. Mary Daly, *The Church and the Second Sex* (New York: Harper & Row, 1968), p. 65.

9. Mary Daly, "The Courage To See," *The Christian Century*, 22 September 1971, p. 1108.

10. Mary Daly, *Beyond God the Father: Toward a Philosophy of Women's Liberation* (Boston: Beacon Press, 1973), p. 9.

11. Ibid., p. 96.

12. Mary Daly, *The Church and the Second Sex*, rev. ed. (New York: Harper & Row, 1975), p. 6.

13. Ibid., p. 49.

14. Mary Daly, *Gyn/Ecology: The Metaethics of Radical Feminism* (Boston: Beacon Press, 1978), p. xi.

15. Ibid., p. 29.

16. Ibid., p. xv, p. 424.

17. Mary Daly, "The Qualitative Leap Beyond Patriarchal Religion," *Quest*, Spring 1975, p. 32.

18. Rosemary Ruether, *New Woman, New Earth: Sexist Ideologies and Human Liberation* (New York: The Seabury Press, 1975), p. 121.

19. Rosemary Ruether, ed., *Liberation Theology* (New York: Paulist Press, 1972), p. 13.

20. Ruether, *New Woman, New Earth*, pp. xi, 125.

21. Rosemary Ruether, *The Christian Century*, 2 April 1980, p. 378.

22. Carter Heyward, "Ruether and Daly—Theologians: Speaking and Sparking, Building and Burning," in *Christianity and Crisis*, 2 April 1979, p. 66.

23. Letty Russell, *Human Liberation in a Feminist Perspective: A Theology* (Philadelphia: The Westminster Press, 1974), p. 19.

24. Letty Russell, *The Future of Partnership* (Philadelphia: The Westminster Press, 1979), pp. 15–16.

25. Ibid., p. 164.

26. Sheila Collins, "Toward a Feminist Theology," *The Christian Century*, 2 August 1972, p. 796.

27. Sheila Collins, *A Different Heaven and Earth* (Valley Forge, Pennsylvania: Judson Press, 1974), p. 45.

28. Ibid., p. 51.

29. Ibid., p. 140.

30. Judith Plaskow and Joan Romero, eds., *Women and Religion: Papers on the Working Group on Women and Religion, 1972–1974* (Missoula: Scholars Press, 1974), p. 127.

31. Ibid., p. 134.

32. Ruether, *New Woman, New Earth*, p. 58.

33. Ibid., p. 58.

34. Penelope Washbourn, *Becoming Woman: The Quest for Wholeness in Female Experience* (New York: Harper & Row, 1977), p. 2.

35. Ibid., p. 154.

36. Carol Ochs, *Behind the Sex of God: Toward a New Consciousness Transcending Matriarchy and Patriarchy* (Boston: Beacon Press, 1977), pp. 137, 145.

37. Rita M. Gross, ed., *Beyond Androcentrism: New Essays on Women and Religion* (Missoula, Montana: Scholars Press, 1977), p. 30.

38. Naomi Goldenberg, *Changing of the Gods: Feminism and the End of Traditional Religions* (Boston: Beacon Press, 1979), pp. 25, 10, 89.

39. Dana Hiller and Robin Sheets, eds., *Women and Men: The Consequences of Power* (Cincinnati: Office of Women's Studies, 1977), pp. 2–3.

40. Christ and Plaskow, *Womanspirit Rising* (New York: Harper & Row, 1979), p. 9.

41. Ibid., p. 16.

42. Rosemary Ruether, *The Christian Century*, 10–17 September 1980, p. 847.

CHAPTER 6

1. James Barr, *Fundamentalism* (Philadelphia: The Westminster Press, 1977). See also George Marsden, *Fundamentalism and American Culture: The Shaping of Twentieth-Century Evangelicalism* (New York: Oxford University Press, 1981).

2. *Christianity Today*, 21 December, 1979.

3. *Christianity Today*, 27 January, 1978.

4. Sidney Ahlstrom, "From Puritanism to Evangelicalism: A Critical Perspective," *The Evangelicals: What They Believe, Who They Are, Where They Are Changing*, eds., David F. Wells and John D. Woodbridge (Nashville: Abingdon Press, 1975), pp. 270–271.

5. Carl F. H. Henry, *Evangelical Responsibility in Contemporary Theology* (Grand Rapids, Michigan: Eerdmans, 1957), p. 43, p. 66.

6. Richard V. Pierard, *The Unequal Yoke: Evangelical Christianity and Political Conservatism* (New York: J. P. Lippincott, 1970), p. 10.

7. Carl F. H. Henry, ed., *Basic Christian Doctrines* (New York: Holt, Rinehart & Winston, 1962), p. viii.

8. Richard Coleman, *Issues of Theological Warfare: Evangelicals and Liberals* (Grand Rapids, Michigan: Eerdmans, 1972), p. 7.

9. Dean M. Kelley, *Why Conservative Churches Are Growing* (New York: Harper & Row, 1972), p. 176, p. 169.

10. Richard Quebedeaux, *The Worldly Evangelicals* (New York: Harper & Row, 1978), p. 405.

11. *Christianity Today*, 21 December, 1979.

12. Jack Rogers, *Confessions of a Conservative Evangelical* (Philadelphia: The Westminster Press, 1974), pp. 11–12.

13. Ibid., p. 126.

14. Ibid., p. 119.

15. George Ladd, *The New Testament and Criticism* (Grand Rapids, Michigan: Eerdmans, 1967), pp. 14–15.

16. Richard Quebedeaux, *The Young Evangelicals: Revolution in Orthodoxy* (New York: Harper & Row, 1974), p. 1.

17. Ibid., p. 50.

18. Ibid., p. 74.

19. Richard Quebedeaux, *The New Charismatics: The Origins, Development, and Significance of Neo-Pentecostalism* (Garden City, New York: Doubleday, 1976), p. 2.

20. Quebedeaux, *Worldly Evangelicals*, p. 12.

21. Ibid., p. 77.

22. Ibid., p. 100.

23. Ibid., pp. 103, 119.

24. Ibid., p. 166.

25. Richard Quebedeaux, "The Evangelicals: New Trends and Tensions," *Christianity and Crisis*, 20 September 1976, p. 202.

26. Wells, *The Evangelicals*, pp. 181–182.

27. *Christianity and Crisis*, 18 February 1974, p. 23.

28. Ibid., pp. 23–24.

29. John Yoder, *The Politics of Jesus* (Grand Rapids, Michigan: Eerdmans, 1972), p. 250.

30. Carl F. H. Henry, *God, Revelation and Authority*, vol. 1 (Waco, Texas: Word Books, 1976), pp. 121, 164, 232.

31. Jack Rogers, ed., *Biblical Authority* (Waco, Texas: Word Books, 1977), p. 160.

32. Donald Bloesch, *Essentials of Evangelical Theology*, vol. 1: *God, Authority, and Salvation* (New York: Harper & Row, 1978), pp. ix, xi.

33. Bloesch, op. cit., vol. 2: *Life, Ministry and Hope*, 1979, p. 267.

34. Quebedeaux, *Worldly Evangelicals*, p. 34.

35. Barr, *Fundamentalism*, p. 338.

36. Ibid., p. vi.

37. Wells, *The Evangelicals*, p. 187.

38. Carl F. H. Henry, *Evangelicals in Search of Identity* (Waco, Texas: Word Books, 1976), p. 74.

CHAPTER 7

1. Walter M. Abbott, S. J., ed., *The Documents of Vatican II*, trans. Joseph Gallagher et al., (New York: Herder & Herder, 1966), pp. 712–713.

2. John Courtney Murray, *The Problem of God* (New Haven: Yale University Press, 1964).

3. Avery Dulles, *Revelation and the Quest for Unity* (Cleveland: Corpus Press, 1968), p. 283.

4. Edward Schilleheeckx, *God, the Future of Man*, trans. N. D. Smith (New York: Sheed & Ward, 1968).

5. Robert Adolfs, *The Grave of God*, trans. N. D. Smith (New York: Dell, 1967), p. 24.

6. Ibid., p. 66.

7. John N. Kotre, *The Best and Worst of Times: Andrew Greeley and American Catholicism 1900–1975* (Chicago: Nelson-Hall, 1978), p. 96.

8. Leslie Dewart, *The Foundations of Belief* (New York: Herder & Herder, 1969), p. 12.

9. Leslie Dewart, *The Future of Belief* (New York: Herder & Herder, 1966), p. 26.

10. Dewart, *Foundations*, p. 452.

11. Dewart, *Future*, p. 37.

12. Dewart, *Foundations*, p. 114.

13. Ibid., p. 464.

14. Dewart, *Future*, p. 189.

15. Ibid., p. 193.

16. Dewart, *Foundations*, p. 384.

17. Dewart, *Future*, p. 214.

18. Gregory Baum, *Man Becoming* (New York: Herder & Herder, 1970), p. 130.

19. Gregory Baum, *Faith and Doctrine* (Paramus, New Jersey: Newman, 1969), p. 46.

20. Baum, *Man Becoming*, p. xiii.

21. Ibid., p. 170.

22. Ibid., p. 181.

23. Ibid., p. 137.

24. Avery Dulles, *Survival of Dogma* (New York: Doubleday, 1973), p. 13.

25. Ibid., p. 17.

26. Hans Küng, *The Church* (New York: Doubleday, 1967), p. 452.

27. Hans Küng, *Freedom Today* (New York: Sheed & Ward, 1966), p. 147.

28. Hans Küng, *Infallible? An Inquiry* (Garden City, New York: Doubleday, 1971), pp. 15, 186.

29. Hans Küng, *Why Priests: A Proposal for a New Church Ministry* (New York: Doubleday, 1972), pp. 42, 46, 60, 79, 81, 89.

30. Hans Küng, *On Being a Christian* (New York: Doubleday, 1976), pp. 349, 456, 601.

31. Leslie Dewart, quoted in *Critic*, winter 1976, p. 30.

32. David Tracy, *Blessed Rage for Order: The New Pluralism in Theology* (New York: The Seabury Press, 1975), p. 10.

33. Avery Dulles, *The Resilient Church* (Garden City, New York: Doubleday, 1977), pp. 67–68, 69, 78.

34. Bernard Lonergan, *A Second Collection* (Philadelphia: The Westminster Press, 1974), p. 138.

35. The Catholic Theological Society of America, *Human Sexuality* (New York: Paulist Press, 1977), pp. 92–95, 161–162.

36. Karl Rahner, *The Shape of the Church to Come* (New York: The Seabury Press, 1974), p. 73.

37. David Tracy, ed., *Toward Vatican III* (New York: The Seabury Press, 1978), pp. 11, 88.

38. Leonard Swidler, ed., *Consensus in Theology? A Dialogue with Hans Küng and Edward Schillebeeckx* (Philadelphia: The Westminster Press, 1980), p. 68.

39. Richard P. McBrien, "The Roman Catholic Church: Can It Transcend The Crisis?," *The Christian Century*, 17 January 1979, p. 45.

CHAPTER 8

1. Howard Thurman, *Footprints of a Dream* (New York: Harper, 1959), p. 21.

2. Rosemary Ruether, *New Woman, New Earth: Sexist Ideologies and Human Liberation* (New York: The Seabury Press, 1975), p. 125.

3. Robert McAfee Brown, *Theology in a New Key* (Philadelphia: The Westminster Press, 1970), p. 120.

4. Richard Quebedeaux, *Worldly Evangelicals* (New York: Harper & Row, 1978), p. 165.

5. Richard Penaskovic, "Roman Catholic-Lutheran Dialogue," *The Ecumenist*, vol. 17, No. 4, May–June, 1979, p. 54.

6. Raimundo Panikkar, *The Intra-Religious Dialogue* (New York: Paulist Press, 1978), p. 2.

7. Rudolph Bultmann, *Kerygma and Myth* (New York: The Macmillan Co., 1957), p. 12.

8. Peter Berger, *The Heretical Imperative: Contemporary Possibilities of Religious Affirmation* (New York: Doubleday, 1979).

9. Elton Trueblood, *Philosophy of Religion* (New York: Harper, 1957), p. 22.

10. William Pollard, *Science and Faith: Twin Mysteries* (New York: Thomas Nelson, 1970), pp. 79–80.

11. Harvey Cox, *The Secular City*, rev. ed. (New York: Macmillan, 1978), p. 212.

12. Eugene Kennedy, "Karl Rahner: The Quiet Mover of the Catholic Church," *New York Times Magazine*, 23 September 1979, p. 94.

13. William Temple, *Nature, Man and God* (London: The Macmillan Co., 1935), p. 130.

14. Gita Mehta, *Karma Cola: Marketing The Mystic East* (New York: Simon & Schuster, 1979).

15. Carl Raschke, *The Interruption of Eternity: Modern Gnosticism and the Origins of the New Religious Consciousness* (Chicago: Nelson-Hall, 1980).

16. William McLoughlin, *Revivals, Awakenings, and Reform* (Chicago: The University of Chicago Press, 1978), p. 215.

17. Rosemary Ruether, "Motherearth and The Megamachine: A Theology of Liberation in a Feminine, Somatic and Ecological Perspective," *Womanspirit Rising*, eds. Carol Christ and Judith Plaskow (New York: Harper & Row, 1979), pp. 46f.

18. Carol Ochs, *Behind The Sex of God: Toward a New Consciousness Transcending Matriarchy and Patriachy* (Boston: Beacon Press, 1977), p. 137.

19. Sheila Collins, *A Different Heaven and Earth* (Valley Forge, Pennsylvania: Judson Press, 1974), p. 183.

20. John Robinson, *Honest To God* (Philadelphia: The Westminster Press, 1963), p. 29.

21. Alfred North Whitehead, *Science and the Modern World* (New York: Cambridge University Press, 1932), p. 4.

22. Paul Tillich, *The Shaking of the Foundations* (New York: Scribners, 1948), p. 57.

23. William James, *The Varieties of Religious Experience* (New York: Random House, 1902), p. 515.

24. Krister Stendahl, *Harvard Divinity Bulletin*, Autumn 1967, p. 5.

25. James Cone, *Black Theology and Black Power* (New York: The Seabury Press, 1969), p. 35.

26. Gustavo Gutiérrez, *A Theology of Liberation* (Maryknoll, New York: Orbis, 1971), p. 168.

27. Raimundo Panikkar, "The Myth of Pluralism: The Tower of Babel—A Meditation on Non-Violence," *Crosscurrents*, vol. 29, no. 2 (Summer 1979), pp. 199–200.

Suggestions for Further Reading

CHAPTER 1

Baillie, John, ed. *Revelation*. New York: The Macmillan Co., 1937.
Barth, Karl. *The Word of God and the Word of Man*. Chicago: Pilgrim Press, 1928.
Bixler, J. S. *A Faith That Fulfills*. New York: Harper, 1951.
Ferm, Vergilius, ed. *The Protestant Credo*. New York: Philosophical Library, 1953.
Filson, Floyd. *Jesus Christ the Risen Lord*. New York: Abingdon, 1956.
Fosdick, Harry Emerson. *The Power to See It Through*. New York: Harper, 1935.
———. *The Living of These Days*. New York: Harper, 1956.
Kierkegaard, Sören. *The Sickness Unto Death*. New York: Doubleday, 1954.
Machen, J. Gresham. *The Virgin Birth of Christ*. New York: Harper, 1930.
Rauschenbusch, Walter. *A Theology for the Social Gospel*. New York: Abingdon, 1917.

CHAPTER 2

Ahlstrom, Sidney. *A Religious History of the American People*. vols. I and II. New York: Doubleday, 1975.
Allport, Gordon. *The Individual and His Religion*. New York: The Macmillan Co., 1954.
Altizer, Thomas. *The Gospel of Christian Atheism*. Philadelphia: The Westminster Press, 1966.
Berger, Peter. *A Rumor of Angels*. New York: Doubleday, 1969.
Bonhoeffer, Dietrich. *Letters and Papers From Prison*. New York: The Macmillan Co., 1953.
Cobb, John, and Griffin, David Ray, eds. *Process Theology: An Introductory Exposition*. Philadelphia: The Westminster Press, 1976.

168

Cox, Harvey. *The Secular City*. New York: The Macmillan Co., 1965.
──── . *The Feast of Fools*. New York: Harper & Row, 1969.
Gilkey, Langdon. *Naming The Whirlwind: The Renewal of God-Language*. New York: Bobbs-Merrill, 1969.
Hamilton, William. *The New Essence of Christianity*. New York: Association Press, 1961.
──── . *On Taking God Out of the Dictionary*. New York: McGraw-Hill, 1974.
McLoughlin, William. *Revivals, Awakenings and Reform: An Essay on Religion and Social Change in America, 1607–1977*. Chicago: The University of Chicago Press, 1978.
Mehta, Ved. *The New Theologian*. New York: Harper & Row, 1965.
Moltmann, Jürgen. *Theology of Hope*. New York: Harper & Row, 1967.
Mulder, John M., and Wilson, John F., eds. *Religion in American History: Interpretive Essays*. Englewood Cliffs, New Jersey: Prentice-Hall, Inc., 1978.
Ogletree, Thomas. *The Death of God Controversy*. New York: Abingdon Press, 1966.
Pannenberg, Wolfhart. *The Idea of God and Human Freedom*. Philadelphia: The Westminster Press, 1973.
Robinson, John. *Honest to God*. Philadelphia: The Westminster Press, 1963.
Rubenstein, Richard. *After Auschwitz*. Indianapolis, Indiana: Bobbs-Merrill Co., 1966.
Teilhard de Chardin, Pierre. *The Phenomenon of Man*. New York: Harper, 1959.
Tillich, Paul. *The Protestant Era*. Chicago: The University of Chicago Press, 1963.
van Buren, Paul. *The Secular Meaning of the Gospel*. New York: The Macmillan Co., 1963.

CHAPTER 3

Appiah-Kubi, Kofi and Torres, Sergio, eds. *African Theology Enroute*. Maryknoll, New York: Orbis Books, 1979.
Boesak, Allan. "Coming Out of The Wilderness," in Torres, Sergio, and Fabella, Virginia, eds. *The Emergent Gospel: Theology From the Underside of History*. Maryknoll, New York: Orbis Books, 1976.
──── . *Farewell to Innocence: A Social-Ethical Study of Black Theology and Black Power*. Maryknoll, New York: Orbis Books, 1976.
Bruce, Calvin E. and Jones, William R., eds. *Black Theology II: Essays On The Formation and Outreach of Contemporary Black Theology*. Lewisburg, Pennsylvania: Bucknell University Press, 1978.

Cleage, Albert. *The Black Messiah.* New York: Sheed & Ward, 1968.

Cleage, Albert. *Black Christian Nationalism.* New York: William Morrow, 1972.

Cone, Cecil. *The Identity Crisis in Black Theology.* Nashville: African Methodist Episcopal Church, 1975.

Cone, James. *Black Theology and Black Power.* New York: The Seabury Press, 1969.

————. *A Black Theology of Liberation.* New York: J. B. Lippincott Co., 1970.

————. *God of the Oppressed.* New York: The Seabury Press, 1975.

Erskine, Noel Leo. *Decolonizing Theology. A Caribbean Perspective.* Maryknoll, New York: Orbis Books, 1981.

Grier, William and Cobbs, Price. *Black Rage.* New York: Basic Books, 1968.

Jones, Major. *Black Awareness: A Theology of Hope.* Nashville: Abingdon Press, 1971.

————. *Christian Ethics for Black Theology: The Politics of Liberation.* Nashville: Abingdon Press, 1974.

Jones, William. *Is God a White Racist? A Preamble to Black Theology.* New York: Doubleday, 1973.

King, Martin Luther. *Why We Can't Wait.* New York: New American Library, 1964.

Lecky, Robert and Wright, Elliott. *Black Manifesto: Religion, Racism and Reparations.* New York: Sheed & Ward, 1969.

Mays, Benjamin. *Born to Rebel.* New York: Scribners, 1971.

Mitchell, Henry. *Black Belief: Folk Beliefs of Blacks in America.* New York: Harper & Row, 1975.

Paris, Peter. *Black Leaders in Conflict.* New York: Pilgrim Press, 1978.

Roberts, J. Deotis. *Liberation and Reconciliation: A Black Theology.* Philadelphia: The Westminster Press, 1971.

————. *A Black Political Theology.* Philadelphia: The Westminster Press, 1974.

————, and Gardiner, James A., eds. *Quest for a Black Theology.* Philadelphia: Pilgrim Press, 1971.

Salley, Columbus and Behm, Ronald. *Your God Is Too White.* Downers Grove, Illinois: Intervarsity Press, 1971.

Torres, Sergio and Eagleson, John, eds. *Theology in the Americas.* Maryknoll, New York: Orbis Books, 1976.

Traynham, Warner. *Christian Faith in Black and White.* Wakefield, Massachusetts: Parameter Press, 1973.

————. *Black Theology Lecture Series.* St. Petersburg, Florida, 1977. (unpublished)

Washington, Joseph. *Black Religion: The Negro and Christianity in the United States*. Boston: Beacon Press, 1964.

————. *Black and White Power Subreption*. Boston: Beacon Press, 1969.

————. *Black Sects and Cults*. New York: Doubleday, 1972.

Wilmore, Gayraud. *Black Religion and Black Radicalism*. New York: Doubleday, 1972.

———— and Cone, James, eds. *Black Theology: A Documentary History, 1969–1979*. Maryknoll, New York: Orbis Books, 1979.

CHAPTER 4

Alves, Rubem. *A Theology of Human Hope*. New York: World Publishing Co., 1969.

Assmann, Hugo. *Theology for a Nomad Church*. Maryknoll, New York: Orbis Books, 1976.

Bonino, Jose Miguez. *Doing Theology in a Revolutionary Situation*. Philadelphia: Fortress Press, 1975.

Brown, Delwin. *To Set at Liberty. Christian Faith and Human Freedom*. Maryknoll, New York: Orbis Books, 1981.

Brown, Robert McAfee. *Theology in a New Key: Responding to Liberation Themes*. Philadelphia: The Westminster Press, 1978.

Dussel, Enrique. *History and the Theology of Liberation*. Maryknoll, New York: Orbis Books, 1976.

————. *Ethics and the Theology of Liberation*. Maryknoll, New York: Orbis Books, 1978.

Eagleson, John and Scharper, Philip, eds. *Puebla and Beyond: Documentation and Commentary*. Maryknoll, New York: Orbis Books, 1979.

Gibellini, Rosino, ed. *Frontiers of Theology in Latin America*. Maryknoll, New York: Orbis Books, 1979.

Gutiérrez, Gustavo. *A Theology of Liberation*. Maryknoll, New York: Orbis Books, 1971.

McCann, Dennis P. *Christian Realism and Liberation Theology. Practical Theologies in Creative Conflict*. Maryknoll, New York: Orbis Books, 1981.

Marty, Martin and Peerman, Dean, eds. *New Theology No. 6*. New York: Macmillan, 1969.

Ogden, Schubert M. *Faith and Freedom: Toward a Theology of Liberation*. Nashville: Abingdon Press, 1979.

Segundo, Juan Luis. *Liberation of Theology*. Maryknoll, New York: Orbis Books, 1976.

Torres, Sergio and Fabella, Virginia, eds. *The Emergent Gospel*. Maryknoll, New York: Orbis Books, 1976.

———— and Eagleson, John, eds. *Theology in the Americas*. Maryknoll, New York: Orbis Books, 1976.

Wagner, C. Peter. *Latin America Theology: Radical or Evangelical? The Struggle for the Faith in a Young Church*. Grand Rapids, Michigan: Eerdmans, 1970.

CHAPTER 5

Achtemeier, Elizabeth. *The Feminine Crisis in Christian Faith*. Nashville: Abingdon Press, 1965.

Christ, Carol and Plaskow, Judith. *Womanspirit Rising*. New York: Harper & Row, 1979.

Collins, Sheila. *A Different Heaven and Earth*. Valley Forge, Pennsylvania: Judson Press, 1974.

Culver, Elsie Thomas. *Women in the World of Religion*. New York: Doubleday, 1967.

Daly, Mary. *The Church and the Second Sex*. New York: Harper & Row, 1968.

————. *Beyond God the Father: Toward a Philosophy of Women's Liberation*. Boston: Beacon Press, 1973.

————. *Gyn/Ecology: The Metaethics of Radical Feminism*. Boston: Beacon Press, 1978.

Goldenberg, Naomi. *Changing of the Gods: Feminism and the End of Traditional Religions*. Boston: Beacon Press, 1979.

Griffin, Susan. *Woman and Nature: The Roaring Inside Her*. New York: Harper & Row, 1978.

Hearn, Virginia, ed. *Our Struggle to Serve: The Stories of Fifteen Evangelical Women*. Waco, Texas: Word Books, 1979.

Ochs, Carol. *Behind the Sex of God. Toward a New Consciousness Transcending Matriarchy*. Boston: Beacon Press, 1977.

Porterfield, Amanda. *Feminine Spirituality in America: From Sarah Edwards to Martha Graham*. Philadelphia: Temple University Press, 1980.

Ruether, Rosemary, ed. *Liberation Theology*. New York: Paulist Press, 1972.

————. *New Women, New Earth: Sexist Ideologies and Human Liberation*. New York: The Seabury Press, 1975.

———— and McLaughlin, Eleanor. *Women of Spirit: Female Leadership in the Jewish and Christian Traditions*. New York: Simon and Schuster, 1979.

Russell, Letty. *Human Liberation in a Feminist Perspective—A Theology*. Philadelphia: The Westminster Press, 1974.

———. *The Future of Partnership*. Philadelphia: The Westminster Press, 1979.

Starhawk. *The Spiral Dance: A Rebirth of the Ancient Religion of the Great Goddess*. New York: Harper & Row, 1979.

Washbourn, Penelope. *Becoming Woman: The Quest for Wholeness in Female Experience*. New York: Harper & Row, 1977.

CHAPTER 6

Barr, James. *Fundamentalism*. Philadelphia: The Westminster Press, 1977.

Berger, Peter and Neuhaus, Richard, eds. *Against the World, For the World*. New York: The Seabury Press, 1976.

Bloesch, Donald. *Essentials of Evangelical Theology: God, Authority, Salvation*. vol. I, 1978. *Life, Ministry and Hope*. vol. II, 1979. New York: Harper & Row.

Coleman, Richard. *Issues of Theological Warfare: Evangelicals and Liberals*. Grand Rapids, Michigan: Eerdmans, 1972.

Henry, Carl F. H. *Evangelical Responsibility in Contemporary Theology*. Grand Rapids, Michigan: Eerdmans, 1957.

———. *Basic Christian Doctrines*. New York: Holt, Rinehart & Winston, 1962.

———. *Evangelicals in Search of Identity*. Waco, Texas: Word Books, 1976.

———. *God, Revelation and Authority: God Who Speaks and Shows*. 2 vols., 1976. vols. 3 and 4. Waco, Texas: Word Books, 1979.

Kelley, Dean M. *Why Conservative Churches Are Growing*. New York: Harper & Row, 1972.

Ladd, George. *The New Testament and Criticism*. Grand Rapids, Michigan: Eerdmans, 1967.

Marsden, George. *Fundamentalism and American Culture: The Shaping of Twentieth-Century Evangelicalism*. New York: Oxford University Press, 1981.

Pierard, Richard V. *The Unequal Yoke: Evangelical Christianity and Political Conservatism*. New York: J. P. Lippincott, 1970.

Quebedeaux, Richard. *The Young Evangelicals: Revolution in Orthodoxy*. New York: Harper & Row, 1974.

———. *The New Charismatics: The Origins, Development and Significance of Neo-Pentecostalism*. New York: Doubleday, 1976.

———. *The Worldly Evangelicals*. New York: Harper & Row, 1978.

Rogers, Jack. *Confessions of a Conservative Evangelical*. Philadelphia: The Westminster Press, 1974.

———, ed. *Biblical Authority*. Waco, Texas: Word Books, 1977.

Wells, David F., and Woodbridge, John D., eds. *The Evangelicals: What They Believe, Who They Are, Where They Are Changing.* Nashville: Abingdon Press, 1975.

Yoder, John Howard. *The Politics of Jesus.* Grand Rapids, Michigan: Eerdmans, 1972.

CHAPTER 7

Adolfs, Robert. *The Grave of God.* New York: Dell, 1967.

Baum, Gregory. *The Credibility of the Church Today.* New York: Herder & Herder, 1968.

————. *Faith and Doctrine.* Paramus, New Jersey: Newman, 1969.

————. *Man Becoming.* New York: Herder & Herder, 1970.

Dewart, Leslie. *The Future of Belief.* New York: Herder & Herder, 1966.

————. *The Foundations of Belief.* New York: Herder & Herder, 1969.

Dulles, Avery. *The Survival of Dogma.* New York: Doubleday, 1973.

————. *Models of the Church.* New York: Doubleday, 1974.

————. *The Resilient Church.* New York: Doubleday, 1977.

Küng, Hans. *Freedom Today.* New York: Sheed & Ward, 1966.

————. *The Church.* New York: Doubleday, 1967.

————. *Infallible? An Inquiry.* New York: Doubleday, 1971.

————. *Why Priests?* New York: Doubleday, 1972.

————. *On Being a Christian.* New York: Doubleday, 1976.

Lonergan, Bernard. *A Second Collection.* Philadelphia: The Westminster Press, 1974.

————. *Method in Theology.* New York: The Seabury Press, 1979.

Murray, John Courtney. *The Problem of God.* New Haven, Connecticut: Yale University Press, 1964.

Rahner, Karl. *The Shape of the Church to Come.* New York: The Seabury Press, 1974.

Schillebeeckx, Edward. *God, The Future of Man.* New York: Sheed & Ward, 1968.

Swidler, Leonard, ed. *Consensus in Theology? A Dialogue with Hans Küng and Edward Schillebeeckx.* Philadelphia: The Westminster Press, 1980.

Tracy, David. *Blessed Rage for Order: The New Pluralism in Theology.* New York: The Seabury Press, 1975.

————, ed. *Toward Vatican III: The Work That Needs to Be Done.* New York: The Seabury Press, 1978.

CHAPTER 8

Berger, Peter. *The Heretical Imperative: Contemporary Possibilities of Religious Affirmation*. New York: Doubleday, 1979.

James, William. *The Varieties of Religious Experience*. New York: Random House, 1902.

McLoughlin, William. *Revivals, Awakenings, and Reform*. Chicago: The University Press, 1978.

Mehta, Gita. *Karma Cola. Marketing the Mystic East* New York: Simon & Schuster, 1979.

Panikkar, Raimundo. *The Intra-Religious Dialogue*. New York: Paulist Press, 1978.

———. *Cross Currents*, Vol. XXIX, No. 2, Summer 1979.

Raschke, Carl. *The Interruption of Eternity. Modern Gnosticism and the Origins of the New Religious Consciousness*. Chicago: Nelson-Hall, 1980.

Temple, William. *Nature, Man and God*. London: Macmillan Co., 1935.

Thurman, Howard. *Footprints of a Dream*. New York: Harper, 1959.

Whitehead, Alfred North. *Science and the Modern World*. New York: Cambridge University Press, 1932.

INDEX